Rhythm Book 103 Sixteenth Note Rhythm Patterns

Taura Eruera

Rhythm Book 103 Sixteenth Note Rhythm Patterns

Published by Hookmedia Co Ltd

Hookmedia Co Ltd

© Copyright Taura Eruera 2006. All Rights Reserved.

Email: hookmediapublications@gmail.com

National Library of New Zealand

ISBN 978-1-877321-00-9
KINDLE 978-1-877321-01-6

Rhythm Book Series

Rhythm Book 101	Quarter Note Rhythm Patterns. *The Dobodobo Rhythms*
Rhythm Book 102	Eighth Note Rhythm Patterns. *The Dabadaba Rhythms*
Rhythm Book 103	Sixteenth Note Rhythm Patterns. *The Dibidibi Rhythms*
Rhythm Book 104	Triplet Eighth Note Rhythm Patterns. *The Pataka Pataka Rhythms*
Rhythm Book 105	Triplet Eighth Note Rhythm Patterns. The Syncopated *Pataka Pataka* Rhythms
Rhythm Book 106	Quarter Note Rhythm Patterns. *The Dobobo Rhythms*
Rhythm Book 107	Eighth Note Rhythm Patterns. *The Dababa Rhythms*
Rhythm Book 201	Quarter Note Rhythm Patterns. *The Dobodobo Dobodobo Rhythms*
Rhythm Book 202	Eighth Note Rhythm Patterns. *The Dabadaba Dabadaba Rhythms*
Rhythm Book 203	Sixteenth Note Rhythm Patterns. *The Dibidibi Dibidibi Rhythms*

To my brothers, Toka and Poata; neighborhood friends, Grant Hope-Ede and Peter Muriwai, and all the other kids who sang together after school and combed their hair in shop windows and wanted to be the fifth Beatle.

"Dizzy Gillespie said, "You know. Some people think of a note first and then put a rhythm to it. Some people think of a rhythm first and then put a note to it." Then he walked away, leaving you to figure it out for yourself."

Hal Galper Master Class - Rhythm and Syncopation
https://youtu.be/a2XnB5G6oSc?t=2m38s

Reader's Note

If you have not read Rhythm Book 101 Quarter Note Rhythm Patterns

Read Rhythm Book 101 first.

If you have not read Rhythm Book 102 Eighth Note Rhythm Patterns

Read Rhythm Book 102 second. Then read this book: Rhythm Book 103 Sixteenth Note Rhythm Patterns

Contents

Introduction

Welcome to Rhythm Book 103 Sixteenth Note Rhythm Patterns for All Musicians.

In the next twenty-five minutes, or so, you could feasibly read every word--and *talk* every rhythm--in this book. In less than five minutes you can learn a dibidibi vocabulary of sixteen, sixteenth note, rhythms from scratch. Then, in the remaining time, using this vocabulary, you can--to your possible surprise and absolute delight--talk seven hundred and fifty-eight bars of dibidibi rhythms.

This book is a *doing* book. It is not a thinking book. I do not attempt to explain an experience you have not yet had. I give you a rhythm experience first, then, ask you to reflect on what you learned from that.

To that end, my introductory comments will be as brief as possible. As I write I am keeping in mind the question: what is the *least* you need to know to successfully complete this book?

The first point to note is that this whole book is based on only *one rhythm*: the sixteenth note rhythm. This entire book is about talking sixteenth note rhythms *derived* from this one rhythm.

In this book we refer to this seed rhythm as the *dibidibi* rhythm. This parent rhythm is displayed here.

di   bi   di   bi

In this bar you see five horizontal lines (called a stave), a G treble clef, a 1/4 time signature and four, beamed, sixteenth notes or semiquavers. All these aspects are lumped under the heading of music notation.

1

Under the first and third sixteenth notes is the syllable di. Under the second and fourth sixteenth notes is the syllable bi. The vowel, i, in di and bi is pronounced the same as the vowel *sound*, i, in beat. Any syllable displaying under a note is called a rhythmisation syllable.

These syllables form the word dibidibi. Dibidibi is the rhythmisation for a bar of four sixteenth notes.

In the seven hundred and fifty-eight bars that follow I ask you to take no notice of the stave, clef and time signature. I ask you to focus only on the rhythm notes and rhythmisation.

Rhythmisation is to rhythm what solmisation (solfa or solfeggio) is to melodic pitch. Just as do re mi uniquely describes the sound of the first three notes of a major scale so does dibidibi *uniquely* describe a bar, or group, of four sixteenth notes.

Rhythmisation is a system for verbalising rhythm. Rhythmisation is the language we use to talk the dibidibi vocabulary in this book.

The dibidibi *vocabulary* consists of several rhythms *derived* from this seed rhythm.

We concern ourselves with only sixteen of them in this book.

When we talk about dibidibi we are talking about a rhythm *level*. When we talk about the dibidibi's, we are talking about the dibidibi rhythm *vocabulary*. When we talk about a dibidibi rhythm we are talking about any rhythm that is a *member* of this vocabulary.

Talking the sixteen rhythms is simple. **The dibidibi vocabulary uses three vowels** pronounced as follows: i as in beat, a as in bath, o as in go.

As you can see, vowel pronunciation is simple. Pronouncing vowel *duration* or vowel length is not so simple for native English speakers because vowel length is not significant in English conversation.

For example, if you say the word movie, with a really long o sound or short one, the meaning remains the same. The upshot is that learning to talk five different durations--for five different vowels--is a new experience, for most monolingual English speakers.

All vowels are all different lengths.

The **i** vowel is one quarter beat long.

The **a** vowel is one half beat long.

The **o** vowel is one click or one beat long.

The **ia** and **ai** diphthongs are three quarters of a beat long.

Please note that in this book, one metronome click measures one beat.

The consonants, **d**, **b** and **s** are pronounced as normal.

Attacks and Syllables

In any rhythmisation vocabulary, the rhythms are grouped by *attacks*. An attack signals where any rhythm duration starts. Durations may be sounded or not sounded. A *sounded* duration is indicated by any d or b consonant. An *unsounded* duration is indicated by an s consonant. An unsounded duration is called a rest.

The attack status of a rhythm does not count every syllable in a word. Only sounded syllables are counted. This is why *sibidibi* is counted as a three attack rhythm, *sodibi* as a two attack rhythm, *sibia* as a one attack rhythm and *so* as a nil attack rhythm.

The rhythms in the dibidibi vocabulary are presented in groups of 4 attacks, 3 attacks, 2 attacks, 1 attack and 0 attack rhythms.

Dibidibi Vocabulary in Notation and Rhythmisation

Here is the dibidibi vocabulary presented in notation and rhythmisation, grouped by attacks.

The Dibidibi Vocabulary

Rhythmisation by Taura Eruera

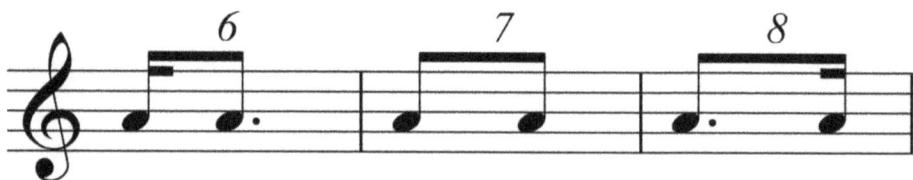

12   13   14   15

do   si bia   sa   ba   sai   bi

0 Attack

16

so

Syncopated Rhythms

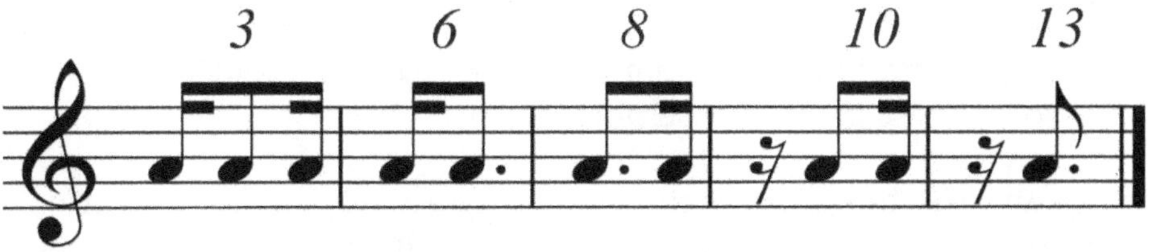

3   6   8   10   13

di ba bi   di bia   dai bi   si ba bi   sibia

Here is the vocabulary presented in rhythmisation only.

4 attacks: dibidibi.

3 attacks: dibiba, dibabi, dadibi, sibidibi

2 attacks: dibia, daba, daibi, sibiba, sibabi, sadibi.

1 attack: do, sibia, saba, saibi

0 attack: so

Syncopated rhythms: dibabi, dibia, daibi, dibiba, dibia

How Do You Learn The Dibidibi Rhythm Words?

Because of the vowel duration challenges mentioned earlier, it is important that you take time to *actually* learn to pronounce each word in the vocabulary. By that, I mean, it's important that your brain *actually* encodes and archives the *pronunciation* of each word *accurately*, that your brain can recall each rhythm word on demand, and that your speech system can *accurately* say each word on demand.

To build this skill, I recommend you turn your metronome on to MM60 and say each word 8 times. If you are saying each dibidibi word for the very first time, focus on relaxing all your speech muscles: lips, tongue and jaw as you accurately articulate each consonant, each vowel duration, each syllable and each rhythm word as a whole.

Notice how it feels to say each dibidibi word once, twice, four and eight times. Saying each word once *is* saying a one bar phrase. Saying it twice *is* saying a two bar, call and response phrase. Saying it four times *is* saying two, two bar, call and response phrases.

Saying any rhythm word eight times is effectively saying four, two bar, call and response phrases, or two, four bar, call and response phrases.

Notice the difference between saying a word on an odd bar and an even bar, a strong bar and a weak bar.

To follow detailed, step by step, instructions, refer to the Learn Sixteen Dibidibi Words in 8 Bar Sections in the appendices after page 104. You can also learn the dibidibi sounds with notation on pages VI-XV of the appendices. At MM60 this process will take you just under five minutes.

Assuming you have learned the vocabulary, you are now ready to talk the big lot of dibidibi's, all seven hundred and fifty-eight of them.

This is not as scary as it might sound. You have already spoken each word a minimum of eight times. Over the next thirteen minutes you will talk each word in the dibidibi vocabulary, several times, in several different contexts.

You will talk dibidibi 32 times across the 758 bars.

You will talk 3 attack rhythms, one hundred and eighty-five times: namely, dibiba 41 times, dibabi 62 times, dadibi 41 times and sibidibi, 41 times.

You will talk 2 attack rhythms, three hundred and twenty-one times: specifically, dibia 65 times, daba 44 times, daibi 64 times, sibiba 38 times, sibabi 66 times and sadibi, 44 times.

You will talk 1 attack rhythms, one hundred and eighty-five times: specifically, do 21 times, bo 20 times, sibia 62 times, saba 41 times and saibi, 41 times. Finally you will talk so 35 times.

You now know a lot. You now know how to *pronounce* each dibidibi word. You know how many times you are going to say each word. You know that you will be talking seven hundred and fifty-eight bars of dibidibi. You know that you will be talking three hundred and sixty-three, two bar, call and response, dibidibi phrases.

You know it will take you thirteen minutes to read seven hundred and fifty-eight bars with no break between chapters (or twenty minutes with energy breaks, or thirty-three minutes with text and energy breaks).

You know it's time for you to now launch yourself. Good luck.

Go talk yourself some dibidibi.

Chapter One: Talk 8 Attack Rhythms

In this chapter you talk only one rhythm: dibidibi, the parent rhythm for this vocabulary. Dibidibi occurs on both the first and second bar, that is, on both the strong and weak bar.

Dibidibi is the seed rhythm that the other fifteen dibidibi rhythms derive from. This is the *fundamental* rhythm that you need to articulate clearly and cleanly. In the initial stages, you will do so carefully and deliberately, then---after many, many repetitions over time---automatically.

In this chapter you want to really feel each beat *subdivision* clearly. Feel each di clearly. Feel each bi clearly. Feel how dobo divides into dibidibi dibidibi. Feel it in your imagination, your speech and your body.

Feel the *strong* beat subdivision clearly. Feel the *weak* beat subdivision clearly. Feel the down beat subdivision clearly. Feel the upbeat subdivision clearly.

Feel the first subdivision on the down of each click clearly.

Clearly feeling each dibidibi subdivision of each beat is fundamental to feeling every rhythm in the dibidibi vocabulary. This is the skill required to be able to feel *diphthong rhythms* like dibia and daibi, and syncopations like dibabi.

Notice the principle of rhythm alternation operating here, at the level of subdivision, beat and bar. Notice what you notice about alternations at the level of subdivision (dibidibi), beat (dobo) and bar (strong-weak) as you talk dibidibi.

This 8 attack dibidibi rhythm has a (4 + 4) rhythm profile. The (4 + 4) profile means that the two bar phrase is a 4 attack rhythm in the strong bar and a 4 attack rhythm in the weak bar.

Notice what is different *within* you as you say this rhythm. How does the strong bar feel to you? How does the weak bar feel to you? Why is dibidibi dibidibi called an 8 attack rhythm?

Chapter Two: Talk 7 Attack Rhythms

In this chapter you are talking 7 attack dibidibi rhythms. That is, all the rhythms in this chapter display a *rhythm density* of 7 attacks. Rhythm density broadly describes how rhythmically active a rhythm phrase is.

You are talking only the first five words of the dibidibi vocabulary--in different combinations—in this chapter. Clearly articulating the dibi alternation you learned in chapter one helps you with talking your first syncopated rhythm in this book: the dibabi rhythm.

In this chapter you are experiencing two bar, call and response phrases. The dibidibi rhythm in the strong, odd numbered bar is the *calling rhythm* while the sixteenth note rhythm in the weak, even numbered bar, is the *responding rhythm*.

The rhythms in section B are called CV rhythms. The CV letters are initials, standing for *constant variable* rhythm which in turn, is shorthand, for a *constant rhythm* calling a *variable rhythm*. That is to say, in section B, a constant rhythm in a strong bar is answered by a variable rhythm in the weak bar.

In section C, the reverse occurs with VC phrasing. That is, a variable rhythm in the strong bar is answered by a constant rhythm in the weak bar.

In this chapter you are also being introduced to the concept of *rhythm profile*. In section B, the rhythm profile of these 7 attack rhythm dibidibi phrases is (4 + 3). This means that there is a 4 attack rhythm being answered by a 3 attack rhythm.

In section C, the dibidibi rhythm profile is (3 + 4): that is, a 3 attack rhythm on the strong bar is being answered by a 4 attack rhythm on the weak bar.

After you have talked these semiquaver rhythm profiles, reflect on how (4 + 3) phrases felt the same and different to you, from (3 + 4) phrases? What did you notice?

7 Attack Rhythm (3+4) VC

11

di   bi   ba   di   bi   di   bi

13

di   ba   bi   di   bi   di   bi

15

da   di   bi   di   bi   di   bi

17

si   bi   di   bi   di   bi   di   bi

Chapter Three: Talk 6 Attack Rhythms

In this chapter you are talking 6 attack rhythms. That is, all the dibidibi rhythms in this chapter display a rhythm density of 6 attacks.

For the first time, you will talk the 2 attack rhythms in this chapter: dibia, daba, daibi, sibiba, sibabi, sadibi; in combination with the 4 attack dibidibi rhythm.

Combining 2 attack rhythms with a 4 attack rhythm will offer you *rhythm balance* insights that (3 + 3) rhythms do not.

In chapter two you met the three attack, dibabi, syncopated rhythm. In this one you meet the two attack, sibabi, syncopated rhythm.

For the first time in this talking section, you are meeting the two important, two attack, diphthong rhythms: dibia and daibi.

These rhythms are two attack derivations of three attack, rhythms: specifically, dibia from dibiba, and daibi from dadibi (see appendices pages XVII-XIX for a detailed discussion of *derived rhythms*).

Repeatedly saying these rhythm pairs---dibiba, dibia and dadibi, daibi--- will guide you to the correct pronunciation for the dibia and daibi diphthongs.

You will also talk more 3 attack phrases, as both CV and VC phrases. You will get lots of practise talking 3 attack dibidibi rhythms. Again, you will reflect on how 3 attack CV phrases feel the same, or different, to you, as 3 attack VC phrases.

At the end of this dibidibi chapter, take a moment to reflect on how, in your experience, (4 + 2) rhythms are similar or different to (2 + 4) rhythms. What do you notice?

How do the (3 + 3) phrases compare and contrast with the (2 + 4) and (4 + 2) phrases. What do you notice?

D 6 Attack 2 Bar (4+2) CV Rhythms

19

di   bi   di   bi   di   bia

21

di   bi   di   bi   da   ba

23

di   bi   di   bi   dai   bi

25

di   bi   di   bi   si   bi   ba

27

di   bi   di   bi   si   ba   bi

29

di   bi   di   bi   sa   di   bi

E   6 Attack 2 Bar (3+3) VC Rhythms

31

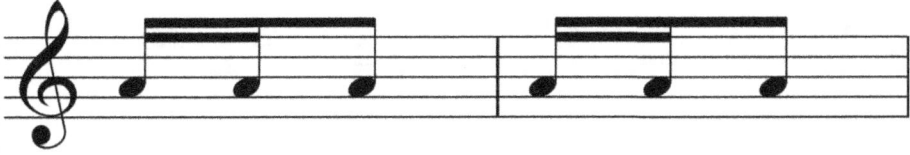

di   bi   ba   di   bi   ba

33

di   ba   bi   di   bi   ba

35

da   di   bi   di   bi   ba

37 si bi di bi di bi ba

39 di bi ba di ba bi

41 di ba bi di ba bi

43 da di bi di ba bi

45 si bi di bi di ba bi

47

di bi ba   da di bi

49

di ba bi   da di bi

51

da di bi   da di bi

53

si bi di bi   da di bi

55

di bi ba   si bi di bi

57

di   ba   bi   si   bi   di   bi

59

da   di   bi   si   bi   di   bi

61

si   bi   di   bi   si   bi   di   bi

F

6 Attack 2 Bar (3+3) CV Rhythms

63

di   bi   ba   di   bi   ba

65

di   bi   ba   di   ba   bi

67
di bi ba da di bi
69
di bi ba si bi di bi
71
di ba bi di bi ba
73
di ba bi di ba bi
75
di ba bi da di bi

77

di ba bi si bi di bi

79

da di bi di bi ba

81

da di bi di ba bi

83

da di bi da di bi

85

da di bi si bi di bi

22

87

si bi di bi di bi ba

89

si bi di bi di ba bi

91

si bi di bi da di bi

93

si bi di bi si bi di bi

G 6 Attack 2 Bar (2+4) VC Rhythms

95

di bia di bi di bi

97

da ba di bi di bi

99

dai bi di bi di bi

101

si bi ba di bi di bi

103

si ba bi di bi di bi

105

sa di bi di bi di bi

Chapter Four: Talk 5 Attack Rhythms

In this chapter you talk only dibidibi rhythms with a rhythm density of 5 attacks.

For the first time, you will talk the 1 attack rhythms in this chapter: do, sibia, saba and saibi; in combination with the 4 attack dibidibi rhythm.

The two diphthong rhythms in this group are 1 attack derivations of 2 attack rhythms: specifically, sibia from dibia, and saibi from daibi. See appendices pages XVII-XIX for details about derived rhythms.

Saying these rhythm pairs repeatedly---dibia, sibia and daibi, saibi---will guide you to the correct pronunciation for the sibia and saibi diphthong rhythms.

Rhythms like sibia, saba and saibi illustrate an important rhythm guideline: *rests are as important as sounded notes*. This ability to articulate rests, is one of the unique features of rhythmisation generally, and of dibidibi, specifically.

This feature protects the beginner dibidibi student from *the common beginner trap*: ignoring rests altogether and focusing only on sounded notes.

In section H you are talking (4 + 1) CV phrases. How does the balance of this dibidibi phrase feel to you when a 4 attack, strong bar, rhythm is answered by a 1 attack, weak bar rhythm?

Conversely, how does a (1 + 4) phrase in section K feel to you? What are the differences and similarities between a (1 + 4) and (4 + 1) dibidibi phrase? How do the differences and similarities feel to you?

Similarly, in your dibidibi experience, how do (3 + 2) VC rhythms in section I compare and contrast with (2 + 3) VC rhythms in section J?

In your view, how do (3 + 2) and (2 + 3) dibidibi rhythms compare, and contrast, with (1 + 4) and (4 + 1) dibidibi rhythms?

5 Attack (4+1) CV Rhythms

107

di bi di bi bo

109

di bi di bi si bia

111

di bi di bi sa ba

113

di bi di bi sai bi

26

5 Attack (3+2) VC Rhythms

115

di   bi   ba   di   bia

117

di   ba   bi   di   bia

119

da   di   bi   di   bia

121

si   bi   di   bi   di   bia

123

di   bi   ba   da   ba

125

di ba bi da ba

127

da di bi da ba

129

si bi di bi da ba

131

di bi ba dai bi

133

di ba bi dai bi

da   di   bi   dai   bi

si   bi   di   bi   dai   bi

di   bi   ba   si   bi   ba

di   ba   bi   si   bi   ba

da   di   bi   si   bi   ba

145

si bi di bi si bi ba

147

di bi ba si ba bi

149

di ba bi si ba bi

151

da di bi si ba bi

153

si bi di bi si ba bi

155

di   bi   ba   sa   di   bi

157

di   ba   bi   sa   di   bi

159

da   di   bi   sa   di   bi

161

si   bi   di   bi   sa   di   bi

5 Attacks (3+2) CV Rhythms

163

di   bi   ba   di   bia

165

di   bi   ba   da   ba

167

di   bi   ba   dai   bi

169

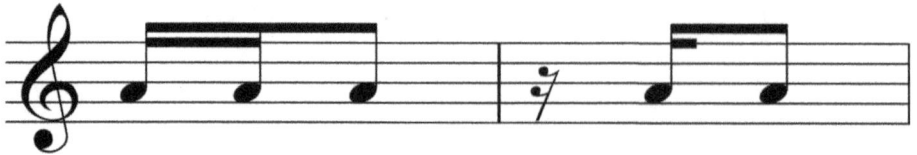

di   bi   ba   si   bi   ba

171

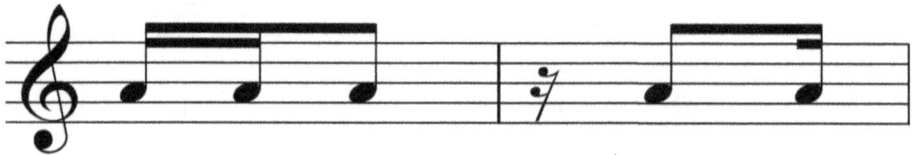

di   bi   ba   si   ba   bi

173

di   bi   ba   sa   di   bi

175

di   ba   bi   di   bia

177

di   ba   bi   da   ba

179

di   ba   bi   dai   bi

181

di ba bi si bi ba

183

di ba bi si ba bi

185

di ba bi sa di bi

187

da di bi di bia

189

da di bi da ba

191

da   di   bi   dai   bi

193

da   di   bi   si   bi   ba

195

da   di   bi   si   ba   bi

197

da   di   bi   sa   di   bi

199

si   bi   di   bi   di   bia

201

si   bi   di   bi   da   ba

203

si   bi   di   bi   dai   bi

205

si   bi   di   bi   si   bi   ba

207

si   bi   di   bi   si   ba   bi

209

si   bi   di   bi   sa   di   bi

Chapter Five: Talk 4 Attack Rhythms

In this chapter you talk dibidibi rhythms with a rhythm density of 4 attacks.

For the first time in this book, you talk the 0 attack rhythm, so: specifically, in the (4 + 0) and (0 + 4) phrases. Again, take particular care in holding the o vowel for a full click. Nothing less than the full value will work.

With the introduction of the so syllable in this chapter, you have now talked all the rhythms in the dibidibi vocabulary. Congratulations. You will meet no more new rhythms in the remainder of this book: just new combinations.

In this chapter you have one hundred, 4 attack, dibidibi phrases, at your disposal. That is, you have ninety-nine *rhythm variations* and substitutions available for any 4 attack rhythm. Through the following profiles, you have one hundred ways to say a 4 attack, dibidibi rhythm.

You have a (4 + 0) and a (0 + 4) phrase.

You have a selection of (3 + 1) CV and (1 + 3) VC phrases.

You have a selection of (2 + 2) VC and (2 + 2) CV phrases

Before you start talking these rhythms, think about what you expect the difference between a (4 + 0), and a (0 + 4), dibidibi rhythm, to feel like to you. Similarly, what differences would you expect to experience with (3 + 1) CV and (1 + 3) VC phrases? Again, what similarities and differences would you expect to experience with (2 + 2) VC and (2 + 2) CV phrases?

After you have talked this dibidibi chapter, reflect on the same questions and see how your expectations lined up (or not) with your actual experience. This before-and-after process is not about finding any objectively right answer. It's about helping you think about rhythm and helping you describe how you think about rhythm.

A parting reminder: with the 1 attack and 2 attack rhythms, give great importance to articulating and saying the *rest* syllables *in full*.

K

5 Attacks (1+4) VC Rhythms

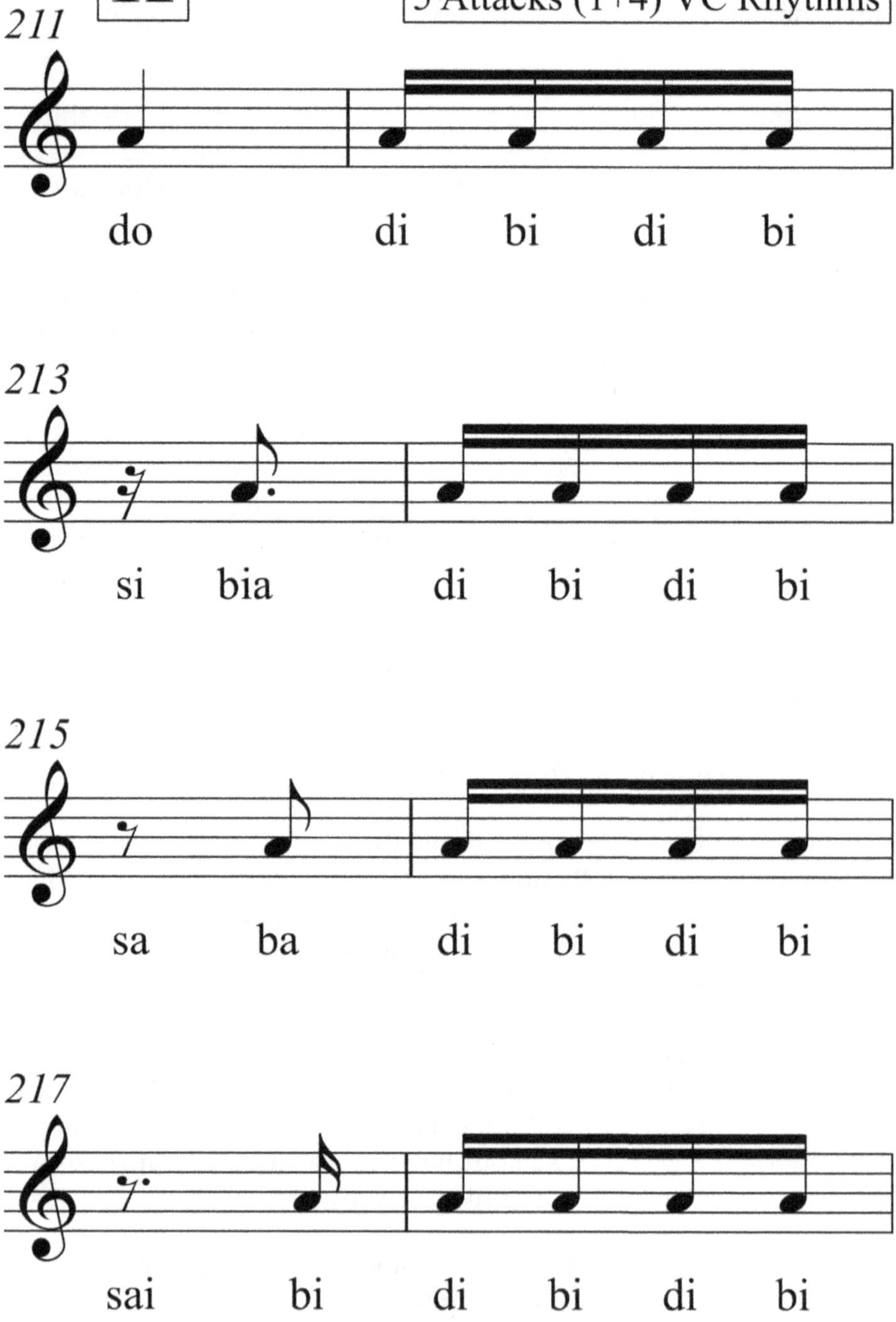

L | 4 Attacks 2 Bar (4+0) Rhythms

219

di   bi   di   bi   so

M | 4 Attacks 2 Bar (3+1) VC Rhythms

221

di   bi   ba   bo

223

di   ba   bi   bo

225

da   di   bi   bo

227

si   bi   di   bi   bo

229

di   bi   ba   si   bia

231

di   ba   bi   si   bia

233

da   di   bi   si   bia

235

si   bi   di   bi   si   bia

237

di   bi   ba   sa   ba

239

di   ba   bi   sa   ba

241

da   di   bi   sa   ba

243

si   bi   di   bi   sa   ba

245

di   bi   ba   sai   bi

247

di   ba   bi   sai   bi

249

da   di   bi   sai   bi

251

si   bi   di   bi   sai   bi

N

4 Attacks 2 Bar (2+2) VC Rhythms

253

di   bia   di   bia

255

da   ba   di   bia

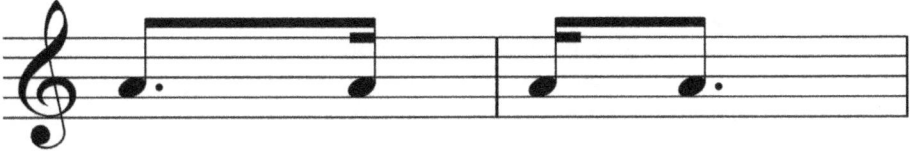

257

dai   bi   di   bia

259

si   bi   ba   di   bia

261

si   ba   bi   di   bia

263

sa   di   bi   di   bia

265

di   bia   da   ba

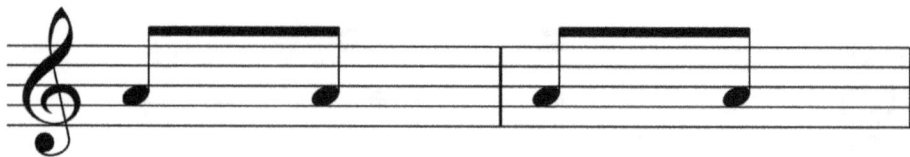

267

da   ba   da   ba

269

dai   bi   da   ba

271

si   bi   ba   da   ba

273

si   ba   bi   da   ba

275

sa   di   bi   da   ba

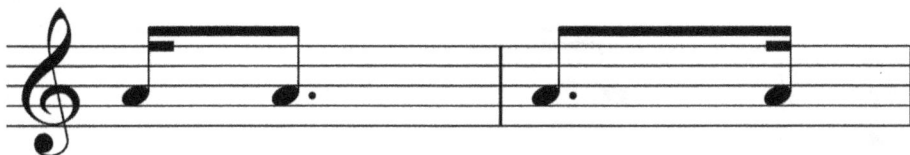

277

di   bia   dai   bi

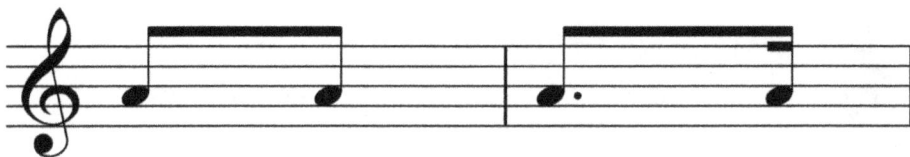

279

da   ba   dai   bi

281

dai   bi   dai   bi

283

si   bi   ba   dai   bi

285

si   ba   bi   dai   bi

287

sa   di   bi   dai   bi

289

di   bia   si   bi   ba

291

da   ba   si   bi   ba

293

dai   bi   si   bi   ba

295

si   bi   ba   si   bi   ba

297

si   ba   bi   si   bi   ba

299

sa   di   bi   si   bi   ba

301

di   bia   si   ba   bi

303

da   ba   si   ba   bi

305

dai   bi   si   ba   bi

307

si   bi   ba   si   ba   bi

309

si   ba   bi   si   ba   bi

311

sa   di   bi   si   ba   bi

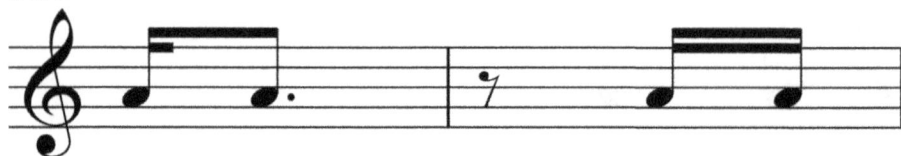

313

di   bia   sa   di   bi

315

da   ba   sa   di   bi

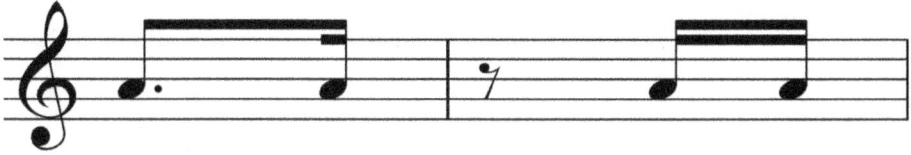

317

dai   bi   sa   di   bi

319

si   bi   ba   sa   di   bi

321

si   ba   bi   sa   di   bi

323

sa   di   bi   sa   di   bi

O

325

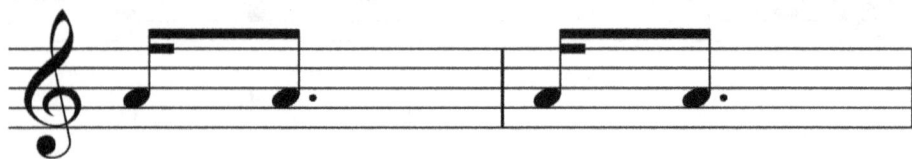

di   bia   di   bia

327

di   bia   da   ba

329

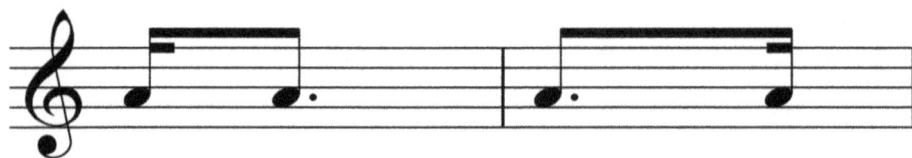

di   bia   dai   bi

331

di   bia   si   bi   ba

333

di   bia   si   ba   bi

335

di   bia   sa   di   bi

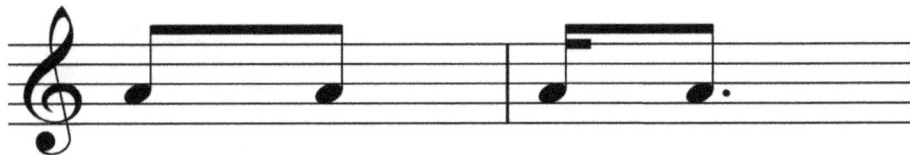

337

da   ba   di   bia

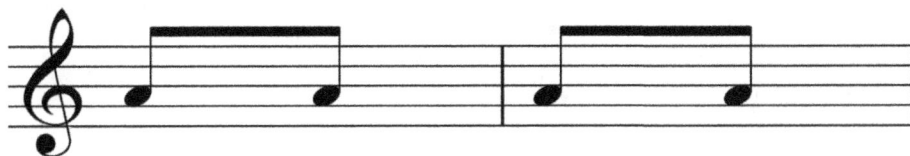

339

da   ba   da   ba

341

da   ba   dai   bi

343

da   ba   si   bi   ba

345

da   ba   si   ba   bi

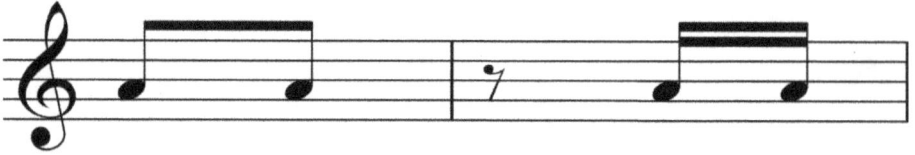

347

da   ba   sa   di   bi

349

dai   bi   di   bia

351

dai   bi   da   ba

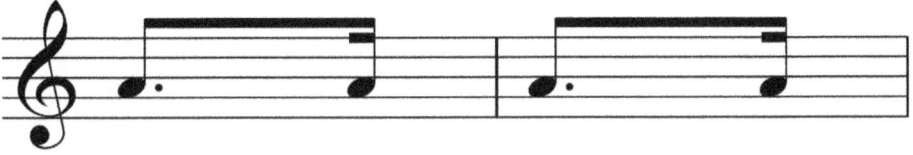

353

dai   bi   dai   bi

355

si   bi   ba   dai   bi

357

si   ba   bi   dai   bi

359

sa   di   bi   si   ba   bi

361

di   bia   si   ba   bi

363

da   ba   si   ba   bi

365

dai   bi   si   ba   bi

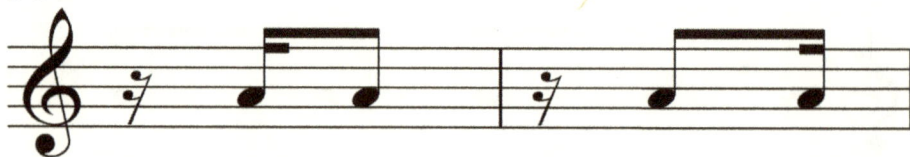

367

si   bi   ba   si   ba   bi

369

si   ba   bi   si   ba   bi

371

si   ba   bi   sa   di   bi

373

sa   di   bi   di   bia

375

sa   di   bi   da   ba

377

sa   di   bi   dai   bi

379

sa   di   bi   si   bi   ba

381

sa   di   bi   si   ba   bi

383

sa   di   bi   sa   di   bi

P

385

4 Attacks 2 Bar (1+3) VC Rhythms

do   di   bi   ba

387

si   bia   di   bi   ba

389

sa   ba   di   bi   ba

391

sai   bi   di   bi   ba

393

do   di   ba   bi

395

si   bia   di   ba   bi

397

sa   ba   di   ba   bi

399

sai   bi   di   ba   bi

do   da di bi

si bia da di bi

sa ba da di bi

sai bi da di bi

do si bi di bi

411

si   bia   si   bi   di   bi

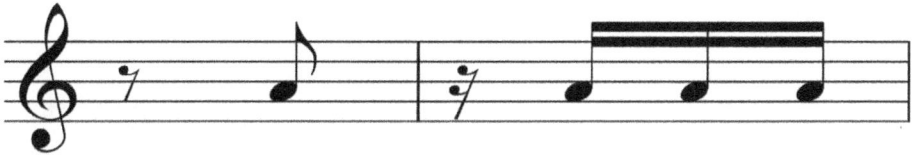

413

sa   ba   si   bi   di   bi

415

sai   bi   si   bi   di   bi

Q

4 Attacks 2 Bar (0+4) Rhythms

417

so   di   bi   di   bi

Chapter Six: Talk 3 Attack Rhythms

In this chapter you will talk two bar, dibidibi, phrases with a rhythm density of 3 attacks.

With 3 attack rhythms, only three dibidibi attacks—out of eight possible dibidibi attacks--are being attacked across two beats. This means that five attacks are not being attacked and that these non-attacked spaces are being taken up with, either, long vowels, diphthongs or rests.

When you talk 3 attack rhythms you are, either, talking attacked long vowels or diphthongs--for their *full* duration—or, talking rested long vowels or diphthongs--for their *full* duration.

Generally speaking, the fewer the attacks employed, the more important the rests are. You must give primacy to accurately articulating the rests, the long vowels and diphthongs to make these rhythms work. Your pronunciation work in previous chapters will help you achieve this skill.

In this chapter you will talk (3 + 0) and (0 + 3) sixteenth note phrases. You will also talk (2 + 1) CV and (1 + 2) VC semiquaver phrases. You will have 58 different ways to express a 3 attack, dibidibi, rhythm. You will have fifty-seven *rhythm substitutions* for, and variations on, any 3 attack, quarter note, rhythm. That's worth remembering any time you have a 3 attack melody to improvise on, or compose variations for.

Before you start talking these dibidibi rhythms, think about what you expect the difference between a (3 + 0) and a (0 + 3) phrase to feel like. Similarly, what differences would you expect to experience with (2 + 1) CV and (1 + 2) VC phrases?

After you have talked this chapter, reflect on the same questions and see how your expectations lined up, or not, with your actual experience. Take note of your dibidibi insights and how they help you think about rhythm in and out of tempo.

The advice to nail the non-attacked, sixteenth note rhythms in this chapter is always worth repeating. Pay close attention to articulating rests and diphthongs *in full*.

R 3 Attacks 1 Bar Rhythms

419

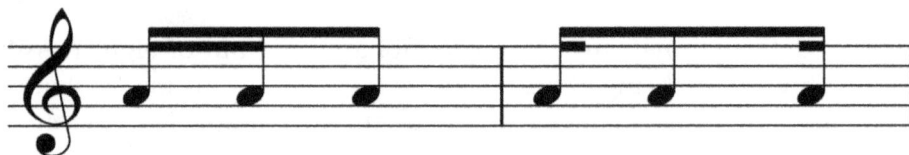

di bi ba di ba bi

421

da di bi si bi di bi

S 3 Attacks 2 Bar (3+0) VC Rhythms

423

di bi ba so

425

di ba bi so

427

da di bi so

429

si   bi   di   bi   so

U

3 Attacks 2 Bar (2+1) CV Rhythms

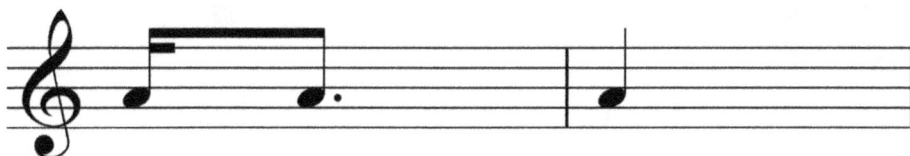

431

di   bia   bo

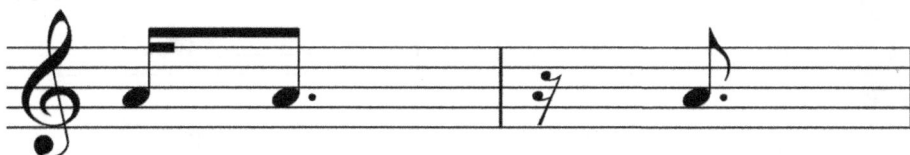

433

di   bia   si   bia

435

di   bia   sa   ba

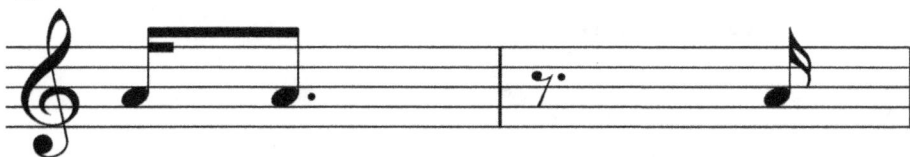

437

di   bia   sai   bi

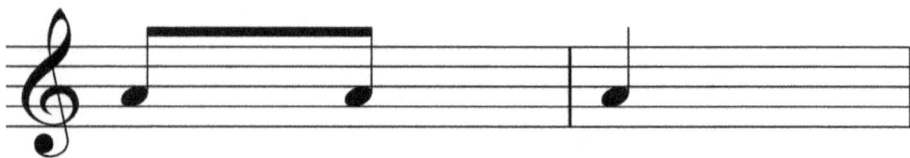

da   ba   bo

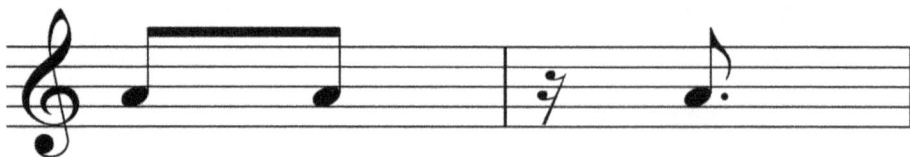

da   ba   si   bia

da   ba   sa   ba

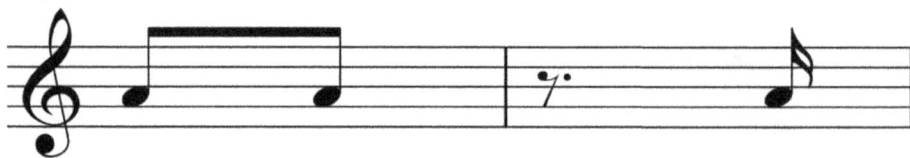

da   ba   sai   bi

dai   bi   bo

dai   bi   si   bia

dai   bi   sa   ba

dai   bi   sai   bi

si   bi   ba   bo

si   bi   ba   si   bia

459

si   bi   ba   sa   ba

461

si   bi   ba   sai   bi

463

si   ba   bi   bo

465

si   ba   bi   si   bia

467

si   ba   bi   sa   ba

469

si ba bi sai bi

471

sa di bi bo

473

sa di bi si bia

475

sa di bi sa ba

477

sa di bi sai bi

U

479

do   di   bia

481

do   da   ba

483

do   dai   bi

485

do   si   bi   ba

487

do   si   ba   bi

489

do   sa   di   bi

491

si   bia   di   bia

493

si   bia   da   ba

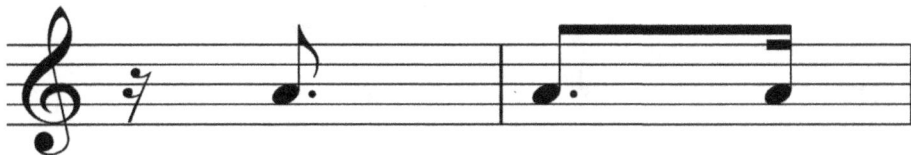

495

si   bia   dai   bi

497

si   bia   si   bi   ba

499

si   bia   si   ba   bi

501

si   bia   sa   di   bi

503

sa   ba   di   bia

505

sa   ba   da   ba

507

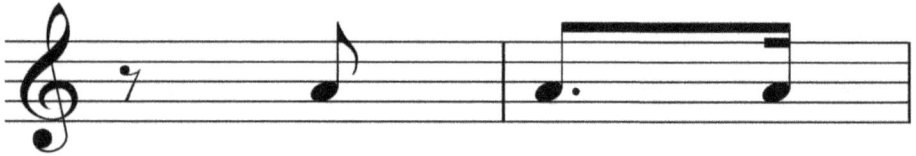

sa   ba   dai   bi

509

sa   ba   si   bi   ba

511

sa   ba   si   ba   bi

513

sa   ba   sa   di   bi

515

sai   bi   di   bia

517

sai   bi   da   ba

519

sai   bi   dai   bi

521

sai   bi   bi ba

523

sai   bi   si ba   bi

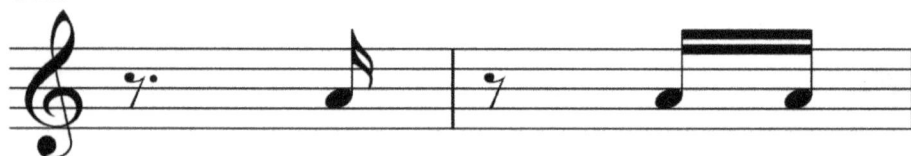

525

sai   bi   sa   di bi

V

3 Attacks 2 Bar (0+3) CV Rhythms

527

so   di   bi   ba

529

so   di   ba   bi

531

so   da   di   bi

533

so   si   bi   di   bi

73

Chapter Seven: Talk 2 Attack Rhythms

In this chapter you talk dibidibi rhythms with a rhythm density of 2 attacks.

This means only two notes per two bar phrase are being attacked while six possible sixteenth notes are not being attacked but are being occupied by long vowels, diphthongs or rests.

With 2 attack rhythms you are, either, talking attacked vowels or diphthongs--for their *full* duration—or, talking rested vowels or diphthongs--for their *full* duration.

With 2 attack rhythms, articulating rests and tied vowels or diphthongs accurately, are *critically* important to making these rhythms work. Fortunately, you met these dibidibi rhythms in chapter two. You have five chapters of experience--articulating two attack rhythms--to offer here.

You met 1 attack rhythms in chapter four. You have two chapters of experience--articulating 1 attack rhythms--to bring to this chapter.

In this dibidibi chapter you will talk (1 + 0) and (0 + 1) phrases. You will also talk (1 + 1) VC and (1 + 1) CV phrases. You will have 94 different ways to express a 2 attack rhythm and ninety-three rhythm substitutes for, and variations on, any 2 attack sixteenth note rhythm.

As you anticipate talking these dibidibi rhythms, think about what you expect the difference between a (2 + 0) and a (0 + 2) rhythm to feel like. Similarly, what differences would you expect to notice with (2 + 1) CV and (1 + 2) VC phrases?

Reflect on the same questions after you have talked this chapter. Do your expectations line up, or not, with your actual dibidibi experience? Notice how your observations help you clarify your thoughts about rhythm.

The advice to nail the rests in this chapter is always worth repeating. Pay close attention to accurately articulating dibidibi rests--*in full*.

2 Attack1 Bar Rhythms

535

di   bia   da   ba

537

dai   bi   si   bi   ba

539

si   ba   bi   sa   di   bi

X

2 Attack2 Bar (2+0) VC Rhythms

541

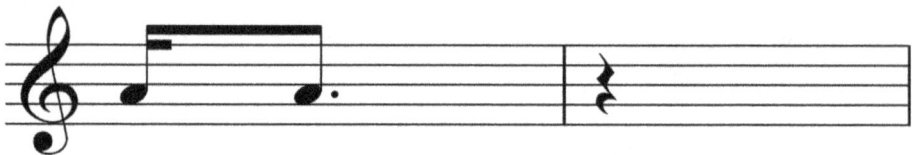

di   bia   so

543

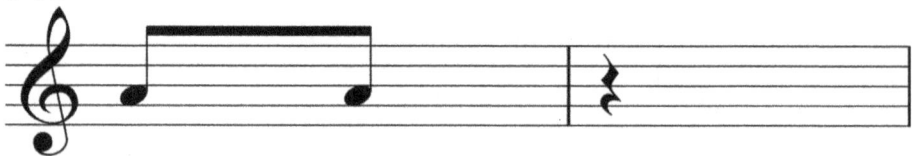

da   ba   so

545

dai   bi   so

547

si   bi   ba   so

549

si   ba   bi   so

551

sa   di   bi   so

Y   2 Attacks 2 Bar (1+1) VC Rhythms

553

do   bo

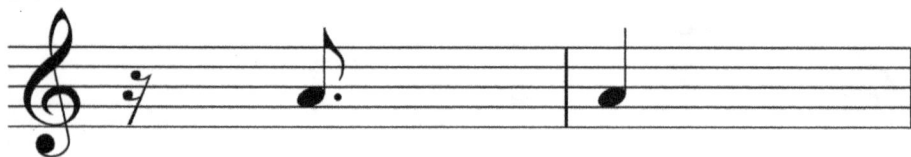

555

si   bia   bo

557

sa   ba   bo

559

sai   bi   -   bo   -

561

do   si   bia

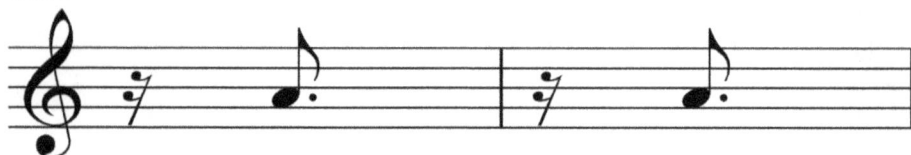

563

si   bia   si   bia

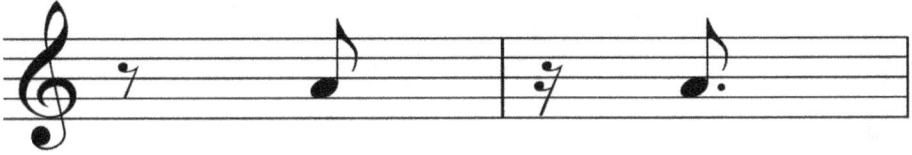

565

sa　　　ba　　　si　　bia

567

sai　　　bi　　　si　　bia

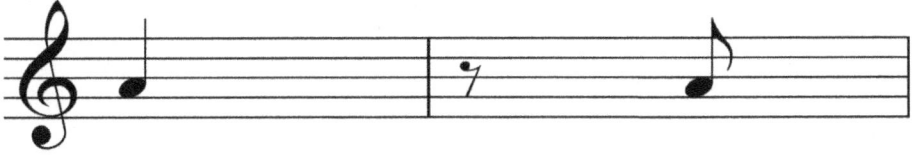

569

do　　　　　sa　　　ba

571

si　　bia　　　sa　　　ba

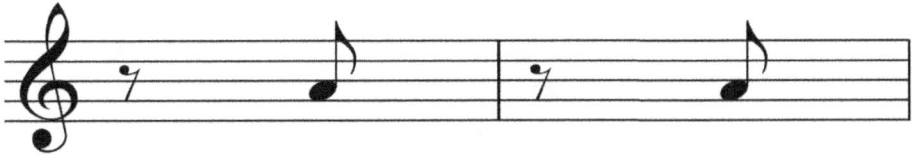

573

sa　　　ba　　　sa　　　ba

sai   bi   sa   ba

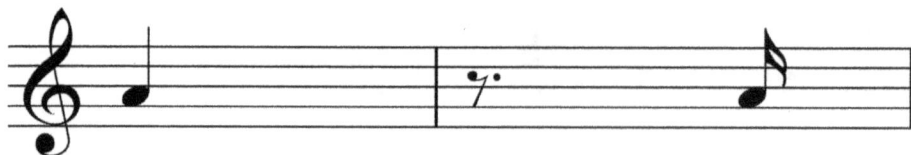

do   sai   bi

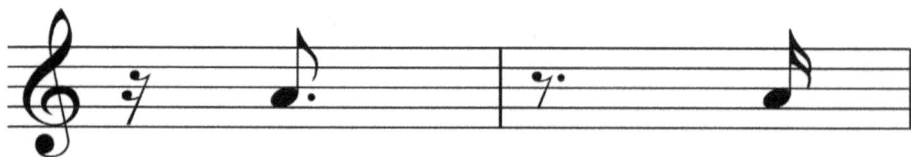

si   bia   sai   bi

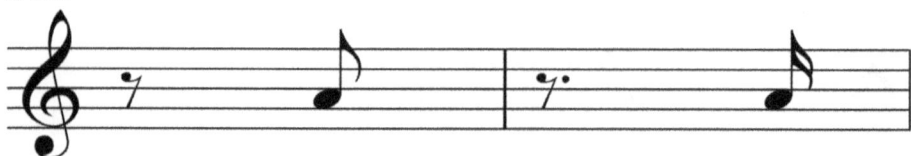

sa   ba   bi

sai   bi   sai   bi

2 Attacks 2 Bar (1+1) CV Rhythms

585

do   bo

587

do   si   bia

589

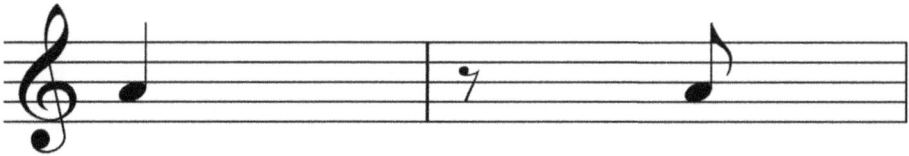

do   sa   ba

591

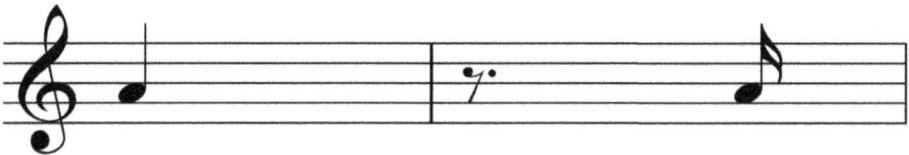

do   sai   bi

593

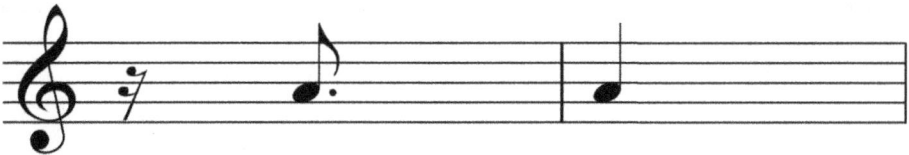

si   bia   bo

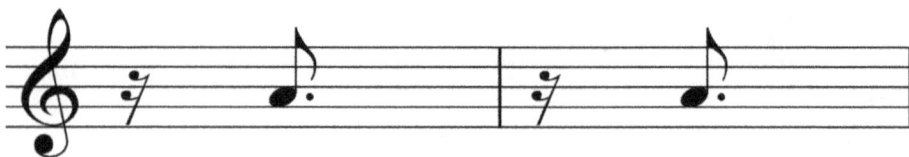

595

si   bia   si   bia

597

si   bia   sa   ba

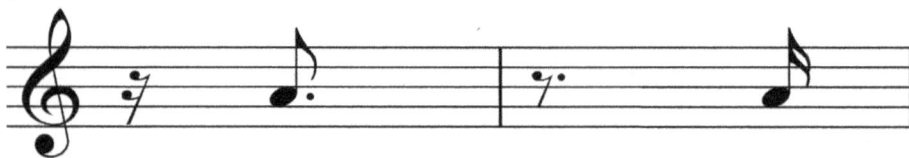

599

si   bia   sai   bi

601

sa   ba   bo

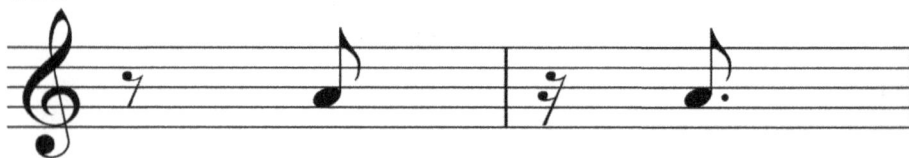

603

sa   ba   si   bia

605

sa   ba   sa   ba

607

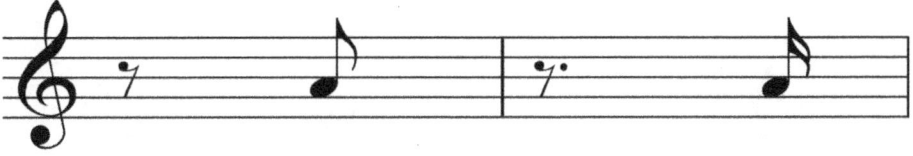

sa   ba   sai   bi

609

sai   bi   bo

611

sai   bi   si   bia

613

sai   bi   sa   ba

615

sai   bi   sai   bi

AA

2 Attack2 Bar (0+2) CV Rhythms

617

so   di   bia

619

so   da   ba

621

so   dai   bi

623

so   si   bi   ba

625

so   si   ba   bi

627

so   sa   di   bi

Chapter Eight: Talk 1 Attack Rhythms

In this chapter you talk, two bar, dibidibi rhythms, with a rhythm density of 1 attack.

When you talk one attack rhythms across two bars, you notice that seven subdivisions are not being attacked and the non-attacked spaces are being occupied with a long vowel, diphthongs or rests.

With 1 attack rhythms you are, either, talking, an attacked long vowel, or diphthongs--for their *full* duration--or holding rested vowels or diphthongs--for their *full* duration.

With 1 attack dibidibi rhythms, articulating rests, tied vowels or diphthongs, are *critically* important to making these rhythms work.

Learning to feel comfortable with the space around 1 attack rhythms is one of the benefits students report to me after working with these rhythms. They also say they are much more aware of rhythm placement when they have only one note to work with.

In this chapter you will talk (1 + 0) and (0 + 1) dibidibi phrases. You will have eight different ways to express a 1 attack rhythm and seven rhythm substitutes for, and variations on, any 1 attack rhythm.

This might be useful to know when you need to come up with a variety of 1 attack rhythm hits for a song arrangement, or, in real time, on your instrument.

As you prepare to talk these dibidibi rhythms, think about what you expect the difference between (1 + 0) and (0 + 1) phrases to feel like.

When you finish talking this dibidibi chapter, reflect on these same questions: Did your expectations line up with your actual experience or not? Did this experience offer you fresh insights about dibidibi rhythm, in and out of tempo?

Pay close attention to articulating dibidibi rests and tied vowels--*in full*. Make the rests so accurate that the single attack just pops right out!

BB

1 Attack 1 Bar Rhythms

629

631   do   bia

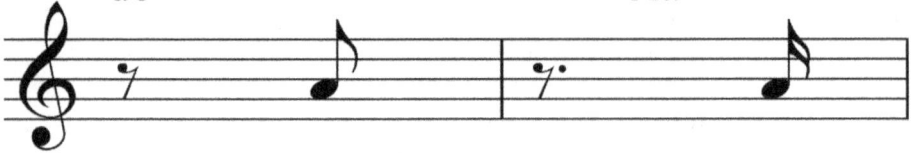

sa   ba   sai   bi

CC

1 Attack 2 Bar (1+0) VC Rhythms

633

do   so

635

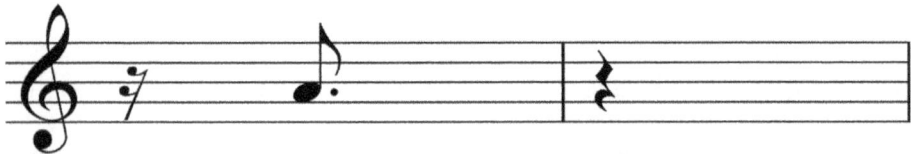

si   bia   so

637

sa   ba   so

639

sai bi so

DD 1 Attack 2 Bar (0+1) CV Rhythms

641

so bo

643

so si bia

645

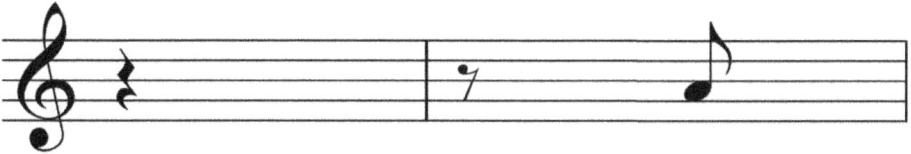

so sa ba

647

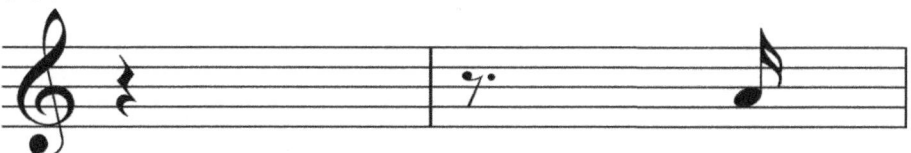

so sai bi

Chapter Nine: Talk Syncopated Rhythms

In this chapter you will talk only syncopated dibidibi rhythms. The five syncopated rhythms, native to the dibidibi vocabulary, isolated for you here, are bars 3, 6, 8, 10 and 13.

You have met all these syncopated dibidibi rhythms in previous chapters. The rhythms are not new to you. However, how they combine with each other, in this chapter, in two bar syncopated phrases, will be.

Although they are not explicitly organised by rhythmic density in this chapter, it is clear that there is one, 3 attack syncopated rhythm; three, 2 attack syncopated rhythms; and one, 1 attack syncopated rhythm

In section EE, there are five variable syncopated, sixteenth note, rhythms occurring in the strong bar while a so rest occupies the weak bar.

In section FF, the variable syncopated rhythm occurs on the strong bar and the constant syncopated rhythm answers in the weak bar.

In section GG, the constant syncopated rhythm occurs on the strong bar and the variable syncopated rhythm answers in the weak bar.

You have these unmarked rhythm profiles available to you in this chapter: (3 + 0), (3 + 1), (3 + 2), (2 + 2), (2 + 2), (2 + 3), (1 + 3) and (0 + 3). You have fifty-five syncopated, dibidibi, phrases available to you in this chapter.

Defining syncopation is not as useful as talking syncopation at this stage. Rather than come up with some definition for syncopation, it's more useful for you to be able to say: "Here are the syncopated rhythms in the dibidibi vocabulary; dibabi, dibia, daibi, sibabi and sibia."

You can say, think and feel these syncopated rhythms, in tempo. You can't do that with a definition.

649

di   ba   bi   so

651
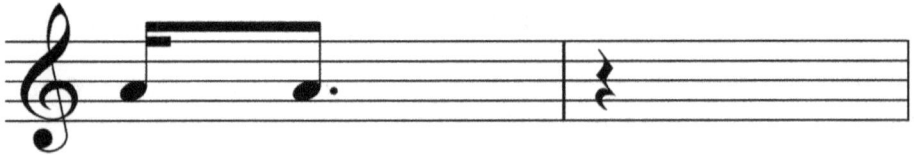

di   bia   so

653

dai   bi   so

655

si   ba   bi   so

657
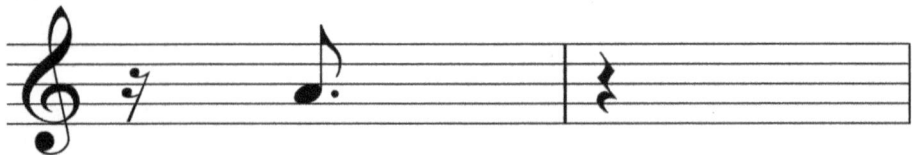

si   bia   so

Repeat Rhythms on weak bars VC

659

di   ba   bi   di   ba   bi

661

di   bia   di   ba   bi

663

dai   bi   di   ba   bi

665

si   ba   bi   di   ba   bi

667

si   bia   di   ba   bi

669

di   ba   bi   di   bia

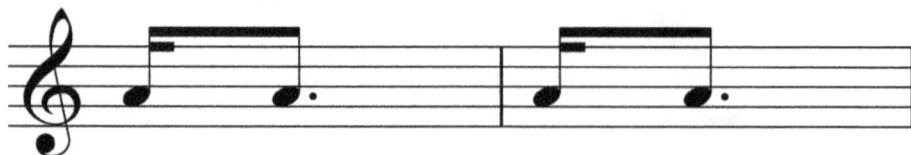

671

di   bia   di   bia

673

dai   bi   di   bia

675

si   ba   bi   di   bia

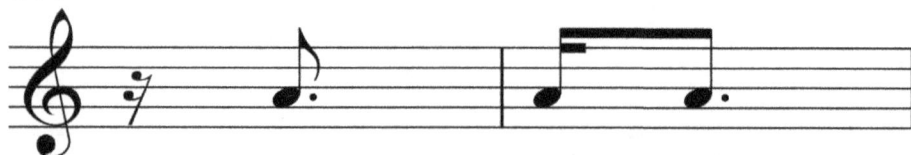

677

si   bia   di   bia

679

di   ba   bi   dai   bi

681

di   bia   dai   bi

683

dai   bi   dai   bi

685

si   ba   bi   dai   bi

687

si   bia   dai   bi

689

di   ba   bi   si   ba   bi

691

di   bia   si   ba   bi

693

dai   bi   si   ba   bi

695

si   ba   bi   si   ba   bi

697

si   bia   si   ba   bi

699

di   ba   bi   si   bia

701

di   bia   si   bia

703

dai   bi   si   bia

705

si   ba   bi   si   bia

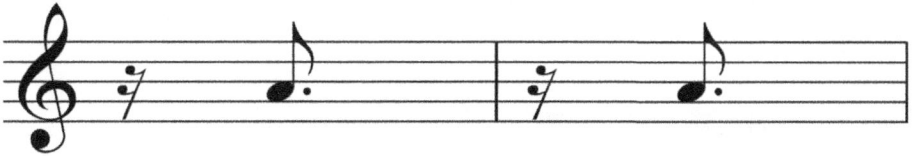

707

si   bia   si   bia

Repeat Rhythm on srong bars CV

709

di   ba   bi   di   ba   bi

711

di   ba   bi   di   bia

713

di   ba   bi   dai   bi

715

di   ba   bi   si   ba   bi

717

di   ba   bi   si   bia

Chapter Ten: What You Have Achieved

In the short time you have spent reading and talking though this rhythm book, you have achieved a lot.

You learned a one bar dibidibi rhythm.

You learned a sixteen word dibidibi sixteenth note vocabulary one word at time. You learned that fifteen of these rhythms derived from the, one bar, dibidibi rhythm.

You learned how much rhythm a simple dibidibi vocabulary can generate. And you talked all 758 dibidibi rhythms.

You talked dibidibi 32 times across the 758 bars.

You talked 3 attack rhythms, one hundred and eighty-five times: namely, dibiba 41 times, dibabi 62 times, dadibi 41 times and sibidibi, 41 times.

You talked 2 attack rhythms, three hundred and twenty-one times: namely, dibia 65 times, daba 44 times, daibi 64 times, sibiba 38 times, sibabi 66 times and sadibi, 44 times.

You talked 1 attack rhythms, one hundred and eighty-five times: namely, do 21 times, bo 20 times, sibia 62 times, saba 41 times and saibi, 41 times. Finally you talked so 35 times.

The net result of all this activity is that you have had a dibidibi experience. You spent 758 bars talking a sixteen bar dibidibi vocabulary in 373 different combinations.

You talked nine chapters of dibidibi rhythms, one **rhythm density** at a time. Within each chapter you talked different **rhythm profiles** and explored all the possibilities within one rhythm density level.

You talked one 8 attack rhythm, eight 7 attack rhythms, forty-four 6 attack rhythms, fifty-six 5 attack rhythms, one hundred 4 attack rhythms, fifty-eight 3 attack rhythms, forty-seven 2 attack rhythms, ten 1 attack rhythms and fifty-five syncopated rhythms.

You learned that each density level could be broken down to **attack profiles**. For example, 7 attack rhythms could be organised at 3 attack plus 4 attack (3 + 4) rhythms and vice versa (4 + 3).

You learned how the principle of **rhythm alternation** (strong bar alternating with weak bar) and the concept of rhythm density can help you predict--and reflect--on the rhythm impact of any phrase.

In short, you have learned and talked the dibidibi's. You are now comfortable cutting and slicing dibidibi sixteen different ways, in 373 different contexts. Congratulations! That is no small skill.

But there's more.

In talking these rhythms you have trained your **ear** to hear these rhythms as dibidibi, rhythmisation words. You have trained your **eye** to see these rhythms as rhythmisation words and as sixteenth note notation. You have trained your **speech** to say them on demand in any dibidibi context.

The next stage is to embed them as physiological rhythm instructions in your body *off* your instrument. The stage after that is to embed them as physiological rhythm instructions in your body *on* your instrument.

The objective of this book though is to *install these rhythms* in your mind and speech and to get you to talk all the rhythms — for your first time--from bar 01 to bar 758. If you have done that then that goal is achieved. Well done.

Now you can read this book again, and again, following along with the section, entitled How Long To Read This Book, on page XX in the appendices. Or, you can proceed directly to talking your way through Rhythm Book 104 Triplet Eighth Note Non Syncopated Rhythm Patterns for All Musicians

Thank you for your interest and time. Thank you for reading this far. Thank you for making dibidibi part of your rhythm foundation.

Appendices

Learn Sixteen Dibidibi Words in 8 bar Sections

In this section you will introduce the sixteen word vocabulary to your mind, brain and speech system. You will teach yourself, step by step, to say the following sixteen words that make up the dibidibi vocabulary.

4 attacks: dibidibi.

3 attacks: dibiba, dibabi, dadibi, sibidibi.

2 attacks: dibia, daba, daibi, sibiba, sibabi, sadibi.

1 attack: do, sibia, saba, saibi.

0 attack: so.

Syncopated rhythms: dibabi, dibia, daibi, dibiba, dibia.

Step 01: Set your metronome to MM60. Pronounce the vowel i as in beat. Say dibidibi 8 times like this. Each dibidibi is articulated across one click.

Dibidibi dibidibi dibidibi dibidibi
Dibidibi dibidibi dibidibi dibidibi

Then rest your mind for 4 clicks. Then take 4 clicks to prepare your mind and speech system to say the next rhythm in the next step.

Step 02: Say daba 8 times like this. Pronounce the a vowel, as in the word, path. Say each daba against one click

Daba daba daba daba
Daba daba daba daba

Then rest your mind for 4 clicks. Then take 4 clicks to prepare your mind and speech system to say the next rhythm in the next step.

Step 03: Say dobo 4 times like this. Pronounce the o vowel, as in the word go. Each syllable is held for one click.

Dobo dobo dobo dobo
Dobo dobo dobo dobo

Then rest your mind for 4 clicks. Then take 4 clicks to prepare your mind and speech system to say the next rhythm in the next step.

Step 04: Say dibiba 8 times like this. Say each dibiba against one click with the di syllable sounding with the click.

Dibiba dibiba dibiba dibiba
dibiba dibiba dibiba dibiba

Then rest your mind for 4 clicks. Then take 4 clicks to prepare your mind and speech system to say the next rhythm in the next step.

Step 05: Say dibabi 8 times like this. Say each dibabi against one click with the di syllable sounding with the click.

Dibabi dibabi dibabi dibabi
Dibabi dibabi dibabi dibabi

Then rest your mind for 4 clicks. Then take 4 clicks to prepare your mind and speech system to say the next rhythm in the next step.

Step 06: Say dadibi 8 times like this. Say each dadibi against one click with the da syllable sounding with the click.

Dadibi dadibi dadibi dadibi
Dadibi dadibi dadibi dadibi

Then rest your mind for 4 clicks. Then take 4 clicks to prepare your mind and speech system to say the next rhythm in the next step.

Step 07: Say sibidibi 8 times like this. Say each sibidibi against one click with the si syllable sounding with the click.

Sibidibi sibidibi sibidibi sibidibi
Sibidibi sibidibi sibidibi sibidibi

Then rest your mind for 4 clicks. Then take 4 clicks to prepare your mind and speech system to say the next rhythm in the next step.

Step 08: Say dibia 8 times like this. Say each dibia against one click with the di syllable sounding with the click.

Dibia dibia dibia dibia
Dibia dibia dibia dibia

Then rest your mind for 4 clicks. Then take 4 clicks to prepare your mind and speech system to say the next rhythm in the next step.

Step 09: Say daibi 8 times like this. Say each daibi against one click with the da syllable sounding with the click.

Daibi daibi daibi daibi
Daibi daibi daibi daibi

Then rest your mind for 4 clicks. Then take 4 clicks to prepare your mind and speech system to say the next rhythm in the next step.

Step 10: Say sibiba 8 times like this. Say each sibiba against one click with the si syllable sounding with the click.

Sibiba sibiba sibiba sibiba
Sibiba sibiba sibiba sibiba

Then rest your mind for 4 clicks. Then take 4 clicks to prepare your mind and speech system to say the next rhythm in the next step.

Step 11: Say sibabi 8 times like this. Say each sibabi against one click with the si syllable sounding with the click.

Sibabi sibabi sibabi sibabi
Sibabi sibabi sibabi sibabi

Then rest your mind for 4 clicks. Then take 4 clicks to prepare your mind and speech system to say the next rhythm in the next step.

Step 12: Say sadibi 8 times like this. Say each sadibi against one click with the sa syllable sounding with the click.

Sadibi sadibi sadibi sadibi
Sadibi sadibi sadibi sadibi

Then rest your mind for 4 clicks. Then take 4 clicks to prepare your mind and speech system to say the next rhythm in the next step.

Step 13: Say sibia 8 times like this. Say each sibia against one click with the si syllable sounding with the click.

Sibia sibia sibia sibia
Sibia sibia sibia sibia

Then rest your mind for 4 clicks. Then take 4 clicks to prepare your mind and speech system to say the next rhythm in the next step.

Step 14: Say saba 8 times like this. Say each saba against one click with the sa syllable sounding with the click.

Saba saba saba saba
Saba saba saba saba

Then rest your mind for 4 clicks. Then take 4 clicks to prepare your mind and speech system to say the next rhythm in the next step.

Step 15: Say saibi 8 times like this. Say each saibi against one click with the sa syllable sounding with the click.

Saibi saibi saibi saibi
Saibi saibi saibi saibi

Then rest your mind for 4 clicks. Then take 4 clicks to prepare your mind and speech system to say the next rhythm in the next step.

Step 16: Say so 8 times like this. Say each so against one click with the s consonant sounding with the click.

So so so so
So so so so

Turn off the metronome. Relax.

Step 17: Take a 2 minute rest. Let your mind wander. Let your subconscious librarians archive all the learning you have just done for convenient retrieval in the future. Let your mind save everything to disc. Acknowledge that you have just done concentrated work and your mind has earned a little rest.

Learn Sixteen Dibidibi Sounds with Notation Instructions

In the following nine pages, you can simply set your metronome to MM60 and read and talk along with the notation and rhythmisation.

The notation guide will take you all of 4 minutes and 6 seconds.

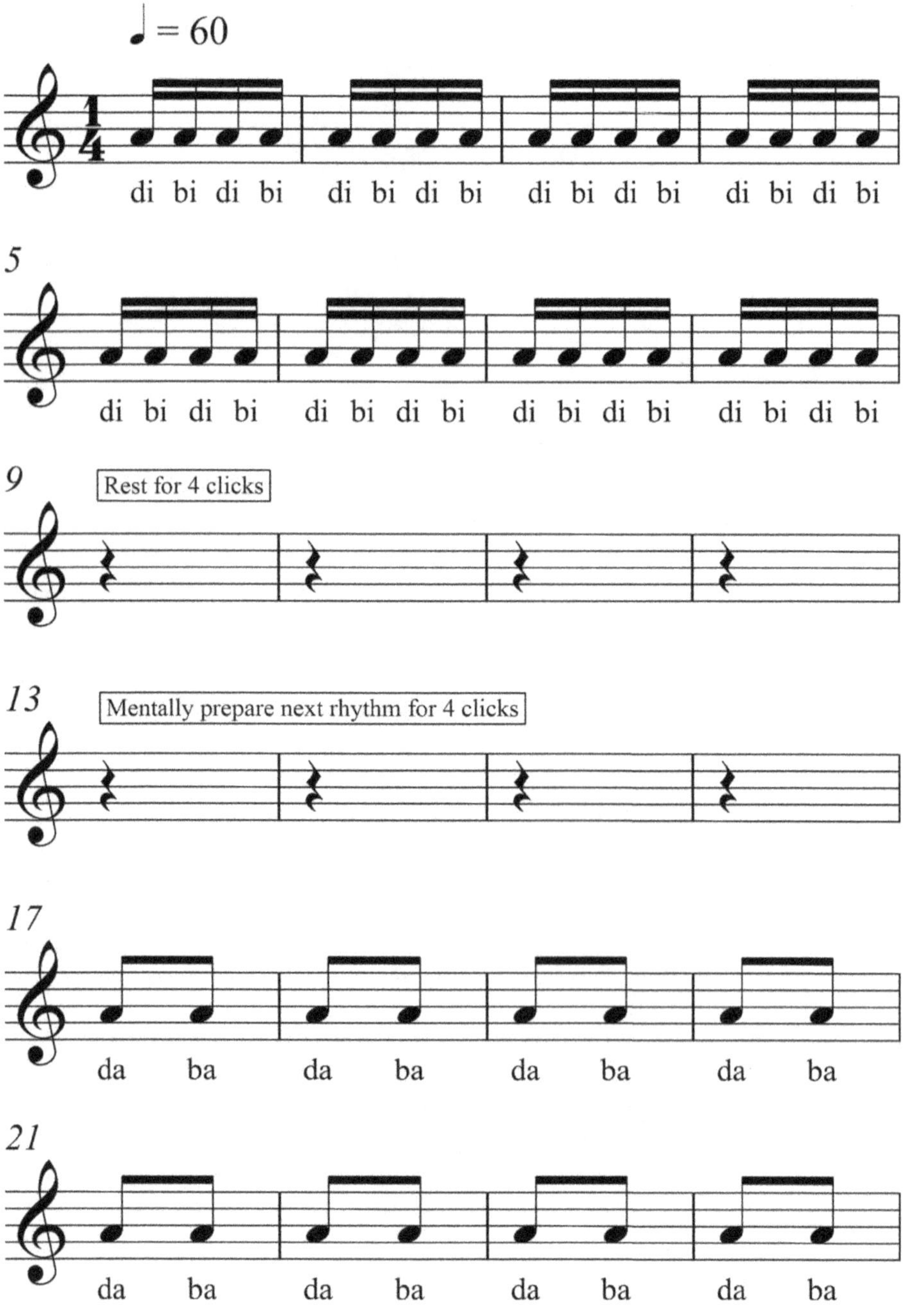
= 60
di bi di bi di bi di bi di bi di bi di bi di bi
5
di bi di bi di bi di bi di bi di bi di bi di bi
9
Rest for 4 clicks
13
Mentally prepare next rhythm for 4 clicks
17
da ba da ba da ba da ba
21
da ba da ba da ba da ba

25

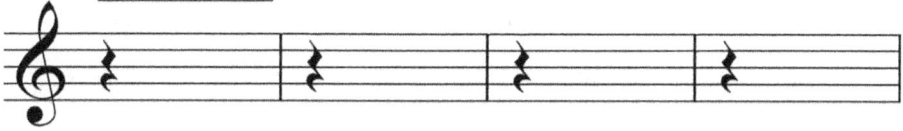

Rest for 4 clicks

29

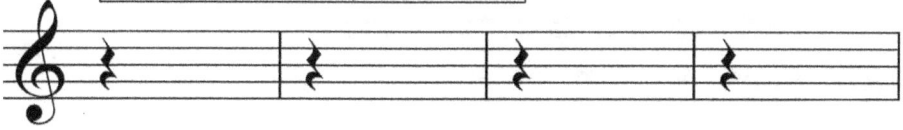

Mentally prepare next rhythm for 4 clicks

33

do   bo   do   bo

37

do   bo   do   bo

41

Rest for 4 clicks

45

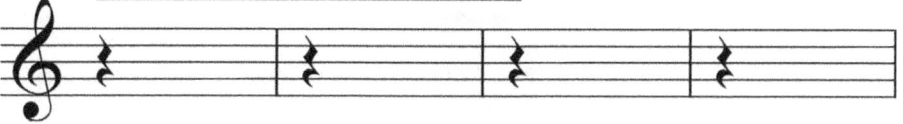

Mentally prepare next rhythm for 4 clicks

49

di bi ba di bi ba di bi ba di bi ba

53

di bi ba di bi ba di bi ba di bi ba

57 Rest for 4 clicks

61 Mentally prepare next rhythm for 4 clicks

65

di ba bi di ba bi di ba bi di ba bi

69

di ba bi di ba bi di ba bi di ba bi

73

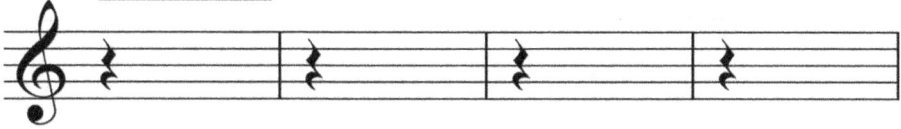

Rest for 4 clicks

77

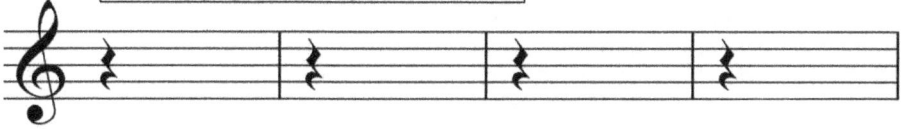

Mentally prepare next rhythm for 4 clicks

81

da   di   bi   da   di   bi   da   di   bi   da   di   bi

85

da   di   bi   da   di   bi   da   di   bi   da   di   bi

89

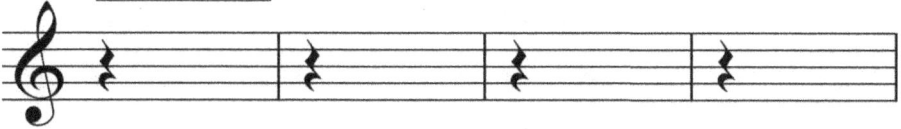

Rest for 4 clicks

93

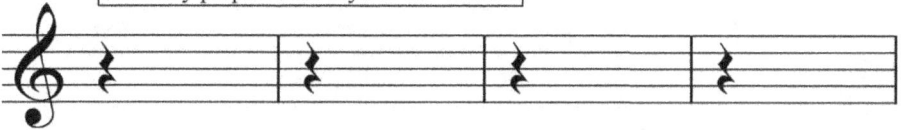

Mentally prepare next rhythm for 4 clicks

97

si bi di bi   si bi di bi   si bi di bi   si bi di bi

101

si bi di bi   si bi di bi   si bi di bi   si bi di bi

105   Rest for 4 clicks

109   Mentally prepare next rhythm for 4 clicks

113

di   bia   di   bia   di   bia   di   bia

117

di   bia   di   bia   di   bia   di   bia

121 Rest for 4 clicks

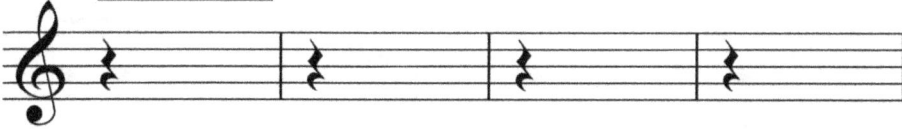

125 Mentally prepare next rhythm for 4 clicks

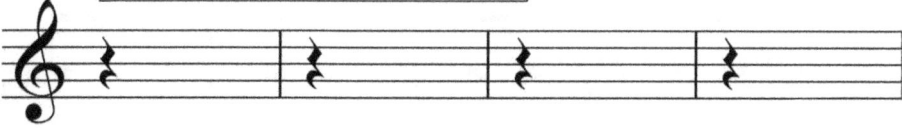

129

dai bi dai bi dai bi dai bi

133

dai bi dai bi dai bi dai bi

137 Rest for 4 clicks

141 Mentally prepare next rhythm for 4 clicks

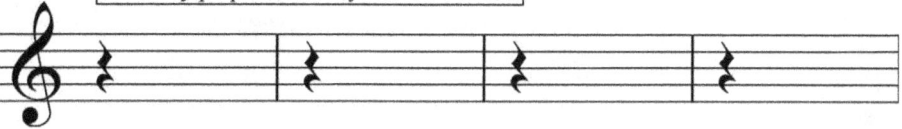

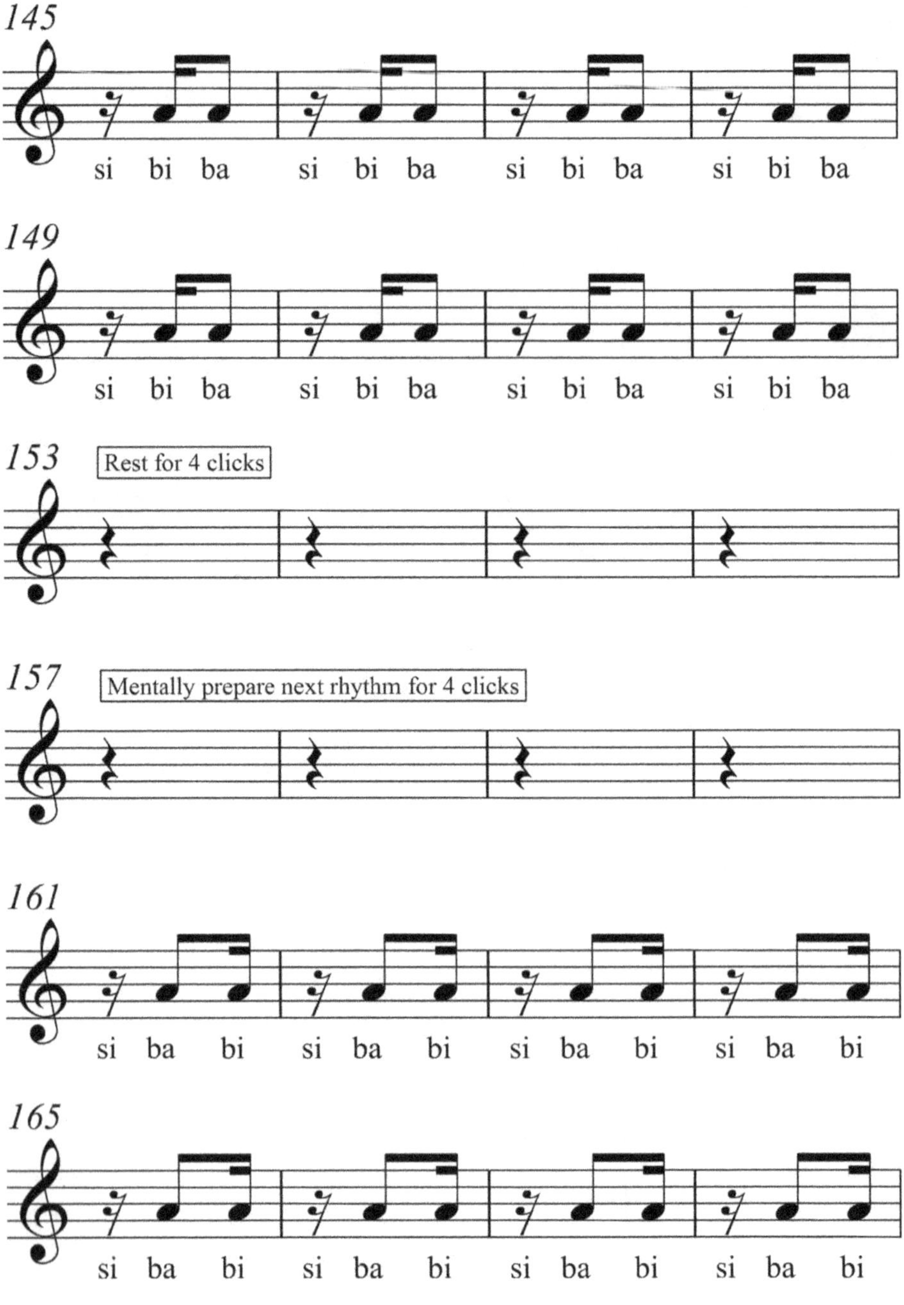

145

si bi ba   si bi ba   si bi ba   si bi ba

149

si bi ba   si bi ba   si bi ba   si bi ba

153 Rest for 4 clicks

157 Mentally prepare next rhythm for 4 clicks

161

si ba bi   si ba bi   si ba bi   si ba bi

165

si ba bi   si ba bi   si ba bi   si ba bi

169

Rest for 4 clicks

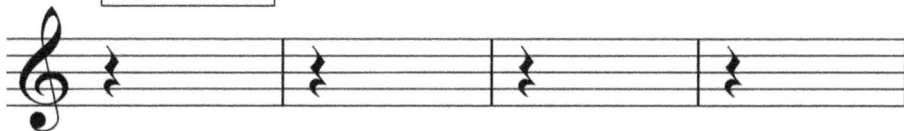

173

Mentally prepare next rhythm for 4 clicks

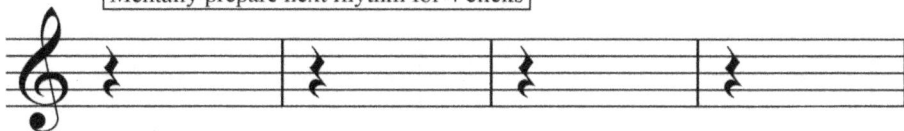

177

sa   di   bi   sa   di   bi   sa   di   bi   sa   di   bi

181

sa   di   bi   sa   di   bi   sa   di   bi   sa   di   bi

185

Rest for 4 clicks

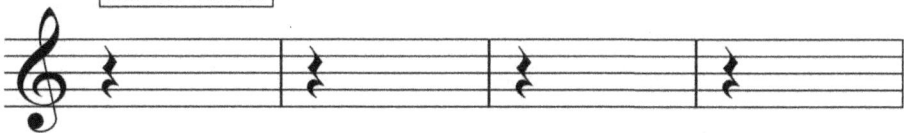

189

Mentally prepare next rhythm for 4 clicks

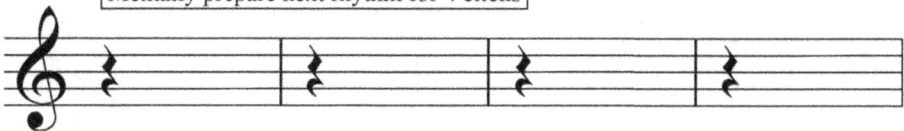

193

si bia   si bia   si bia   si bia

197

si bia   si bia   si bia   si bia

201   Rest for 4 clicks

205   Mentally prepare next rhythm for 4 clicks

209

sa ba   sa ba   sa ba   sa ba

213

sa ba   sa ba   sa ba   sa ba

217

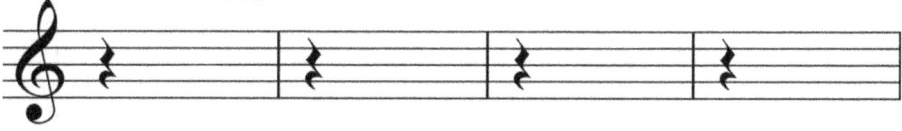

Rest for 4 clicks

221

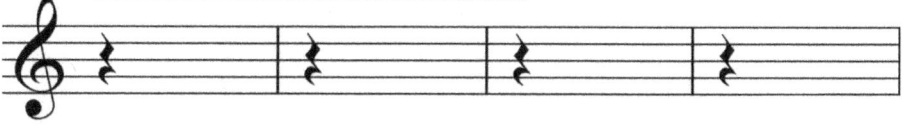

Mentally prepare next rhythm for 4 clicks

225

sai   bi   sai   bi   sai   bi   sai   bi

229

sai   bi   sai   bi   sai   bi   sai   bi

233

Rest for 4 clicks

237

Mentally prepare next rhythm for 4 clicks

Now that you have learned this vocabulary, you can start talking and reading the rhythm phrases section. Or, if you need more work learning the dibidibi words before proceeding, you can do one, or all, of the following three processes.

Learn Sixteen Dibidibi Words in 12 bar Sections

Repeat the previous exercise with 12 bar repetitions instead of 8 bars. The objectives are twofold. One, is to give you practice at isolating and saying each rhythm. Two, to give you experience saying the rhythm within the 12 bar blues form. You will feel a 12 bar form as you say the rhythm 12 times. You will feel the form as well as the surface rhythm. When you can feel a song form, it makes getting lost in any song, very difficult.

Learn Sixteen Dibidibi Words in 16 bar Sections

Repeat the previous exercise with 16 repetitions instead of 12. The objectives are twofold. One is to give you practise at isolating and saying each rhythm. Two, is to give you experience saying the rhythm within a sixteen bar form. Sixteen bars is typically the length of two verses or a bridge and last verse in typical standard jazz and pop tunes. Again you are feeling form as well as surface rhythm. Very cool.

Learn Sixteen Dibidibi Words in 32 bar Sections

Repeat the previous exercise with 32 repetitions instead of 16 bars. The objectives are twofold. One is to give you practise at isolating and saying each rhythm. Two, is to give you experience saying the rhythm within a thirty two bar form. Thirty two bars is the typical length of a standard jazz and pop tune. Again you are feeling form as well as surface rhythm when you repeat any dibidibi rhythm 32 times.

A Note About Bar Lengths

In Rhythm 101 and Rhythm Book 102 the bar lengths for these three exercises, were 4/4 and 2/4 respectively. The bars in this book are 1/4 bars. These 1/4 bars are a learning tool to help you isolate each dibidibi rhythm. 1/4 bars rarely occur in the literature.

If you want these exercises to simulate 4/4 then you will need to talk the dibidibi's in 48 bar sections rather than twelve, 64 bar sections rather than sixteen, and 128 bar sections rather than thirty two bars.

Frequently Asked Questions

Why does saying the d and b in the prescribed place matter?

Whenever you say di, da, do, du you are saying a *rhythm event* that starts on the strong beat subdivision, the strong beat division, the strong beat, the strong half of the bar or on the strong bar. Whenever you say bi, ba, bo, bu you are saying an event that starts on the weak beat subdivision, the weak beat division, the weak beat, the weak half of the bar or on the weak bar.

By specifying whether any rhythm is a weak or strong event (the same rhythm can be weak or strong) you are aware of the principle of rhythmic alternation (between strong and weak events) operating. Knowing whether events are weak or strong enables you to feel surface and underlying rhythm *simultaneously*.

In short, the specific d and b consonants are signposts that prevent you from getting lost in any music you are playing. And when you do get lost, they help you find your place again quicker.

How does saying the d and b in the prescribed place help a rhythm guitar player?

Any d led syllable means you down pick or down strum that syllable. Any b led syllable means you up pick or up strum that syllable. In other words, the consonants are specific picking and strumming instructions.

How is each rhythm derived from dibidibi?

Each surface dibidibi rhythm is related to the underlying dibidibi rhythm by between one to six steps.

I'll simply list each rhythm and their derivations from dibidibi to surface rhythm.

I'll walk you through the steps for two of the sixteen rhythms.

XVII

Example 01: dibidibi > dibi_ibi > dibiibi >dibabi

For the dibabi rhythm, start with dibidibi, remove the third consonant to read dibi_ibi, combine i_i into ii then rewrite ii as an a vowel to now read dibabi.

Example 02: dibidibi > di_idi_i > diidii > dada > daba

For the daba rhythm, start with dibidibi, remove the second and fourth consonants to now read di_idi_i, rewrite i_i as ii then rewrite ii as a vowel to now read dada, then comply with the principle of alternation and rewrite as daba

Here are the remaining dibidibi rhythms with their derivations from dibidibi.

3 attack rhythms

dibidibi > dibidi_i > dibidii > dibida > dibiba >

dibidibi > dibi_ibi > dibiibi > dibabi

dibidibi > di_idibi > diidibi > dadibi

dibidibi > sibidibi

2 attack rhythms

dibidibi > dibi_i_i > dibi_ii > dibi_a > dibia

dibidibi > di_idi_i > diidii > dada > daba

dibidibi > di_i_ibi > dii_ibi > da_ibi > daibi

dibidibi > dibidi_i > dibidii > dibida > dibiba > sibiba

dibidibi > dibi_ibi > dibiibi > dibabi > sibabi

dibidibi > di_idibi > diidibi > dadibi > sadibi

1 attack rhythms

dibidibi > di_i_ i _i > da_ii > da_a > daa > du

dibidibi > dibi_i_i > dibi_ii > dibi_a > dibia > sibia

dibidibi > di_idi_i > diidii > dada > daba > saba

dibidibi > di_i_ibi > dii_ibi > da_ibi > daibi > saibi >

These derivations give you a detailed understanding of how each rhythm derives from dibidibi, how they all belong to the dibidibi vocabulary and in what *specific* sense they can each be called a dibidibi rhythm.

Do I keep the tempo in my hands or feet?

Keep the tempo in your feet. Keep the *melodic rhythm* in your speech and/or hands. In this book you are talking melodic rhythm.

What tempo rhythm should I use?

You want to play dobodobo rhythm in your feet while you talk dibidibi. This is how you most want to keep tempo. Firstly, with a metronome set to a dobodobo tempo, play dobodobo rhythm tempo in your feet, while you talk dibidibi. Secondly, repeat the same process without a metronome.

If you can play dubu in your feet while you talk dibidibi, then you are talking serious rhythm skills. Otherwise, playing dobo in your feet against spoken dibidibi is great.

How long to read the whole book?

Good news. This book takes you half the time it took you to read Rhythm Book 102 and one quarter of the time it took you to read Rhythm Book 101. Why? Because the bar length in this book is 1/4 compared to the bars of 2/4 in Rhythm Book 102 as against bars of 4/4 in the Rhythm Book 101.

At a continuous tempo of MM60 it would take you 12 minutes 38 seconds to read every single bar the first time.

This book contains 758 beats of notation and rhythmisation. Your first task is to read through the book once. Then, periodically read, talk and play all the chapters, one to ten, one session at a time.

This table below outlines how long (to the nearest minute) each session will take you at any given tempo. Take your time. Enjoy.

Example:
At a continuous tempo of MM84 it would take you 9 minutes to read every single bar.

Tempo	Minutes
MM 60	13
MM 64	12
MM 68	11
MM 72	11
MM 76	10
MM 80	10
MM 84	9
MM 88	9
MM 92	8
MM 96	8
MM 100	8
MM 104	7
MM 108	7
MM 112	7
MM 116	6
MM 120	6
MM 124	6

Do you count rhythm with rhythmisation?

Counting rhythm is one rhythm learning and measuring system and rhythmisation is another. You can use both systems. The author uses rhythm counting for *out* of tempo analysis and measurement of *static rhythm*. For *in* tempo *dynamic* rhythm description and articulation, he uses rhythmisation. The author uses rhythmisation over ninety-five percent of the time, and counting, the other five percent of the time.

Rhythm counting describes only the attack and not the duration of any rhythm. Rhythmisation describes both. Saying any rhythm word with the correct vowel duration *automatically* gives you the correct rhythm.

Is Rhythmisation the only rhythm verbalisation system?

No. There are several others some new, some centuries old. The Carnatic vocal system of Konnokol or Solkattu is a rhythm verbalisation system. In her 1998 Masters in Music Performance thesis entitled "KONNAKOL The History and Development of Solkattu - the Vocal Syllables - of the Mridangam", Lisa Young gives you a well documented introduction. For more information, visit www.lisayoung.com.au

Another verbalisation system gaining traction in the west is Takadimi. The Takadimi system of rhythm pedagogy is described in "Takadimi: A Beat-Oriented System of Rhythm Pedagogy," Journal of Music Theory Pedagogy, 1996, by Hoffman, Pelto, and White. For more information, visit www.takadimi.net.

Rhythmisation was first taught in Auckland, New Zealand in 1982, some 14 years before the cited Konnokol and Takadimi works were published and 17 years before the author gained dial up internet access in 1999.

Some African rhythm verbalisation traditions are described in African Rhythm and African Sensibility, by John Miller Chernoff.

There are other rhythmisation systems used in primary and secondary schools including Kodaly, Orff and Edward E. Gordon, amongst others.

How does knowing Dobodobo help the jazz, rock and pop musician?

Dobodobo is the beat rhythm in western commercial music. The first thing you need to be able to do is keep the beat, in its simple and derived forms. Being able to keep the beat through any dobodobo rhythm is the most basic commercial, and social, music skill required.

Rockers, jazzers and pop musicians deal mostly in the dabadaba eighth note melodic rhythms. These are divisions of what? They are divisions of the dobodobo or quarter note rhythm. When you know your dobodobo's you can divide them. When you don't know them you can't. The most convincing dibidibi rhythm performances are those supported by a strong dobodobo foundation. The wimpiest eighth note rhythm performances are those that are not founded on a strong dobodobo framework.

How does knowing Dobodobo help the blues and reggae musician?

Blues and reggae styles are largely characterised by dibidibi melodic rhythms. Dibidibi rhythms are divisions of the dabadaba rhythms and subdivisions of the dobodobo rhythms. When you know your dobodobo's you can divide them into dabadaba eighth notes and subdivide them further into dibidibi sixteenth notes. The most convincing dibidibi performances are those supported by a strong dabadaba framework which is, in turn, supported by a strong dobodobo framework. The wimpiest sixteenth note rhythm performances are those that are not supported by a strong dabadaba framework, which, in turn, are not supported by a strong dobodobo framework

How does Dobodobo help understanding odd beat subdivisions?

Dobodobo provides you with the framework you need to be subdivide any quarter note into any triplet, quintuplet and septuplet value.

What is the principle of rhythmic alternation?

Alternation in music reflects alternations that occur in the natural world: alternating tides coming in and out, sun rising and setting, moon rising and setting, up and down, happy and sad and so on.

The key rhythmic alternation in music is strong versus weak.

Strong (odd numbered) bars versus weak (even numbered) bars. Strong (odd numbered) beats versus weak (even numbered) beats: on the beat versus off the beat; downbeat versus the upbeat.

Strong beat divisions versus weak beat divisions. Strong beat subdivisions versus weak beat subdivisions:

The hierarchy of strong-weak rhythmic alternations is displayed here.

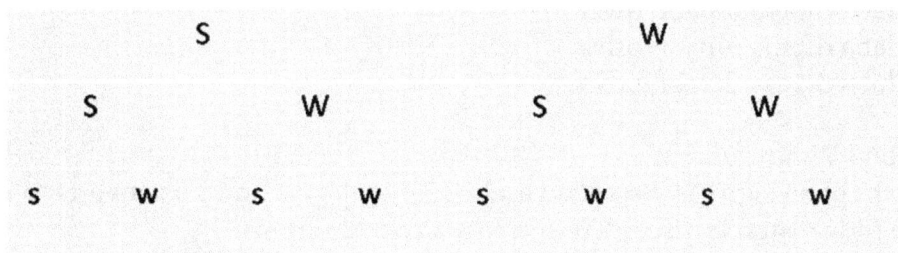

		S				W	
S			W	S			W
S	W	S	W	S	W	S	W

For the purposes of the dibidibi's you can think of the three S W levels from top to bottom as representing do bo, dividing into da ba, da ba, subdividing into di bi di bi di bi di bi, as illustrated below.

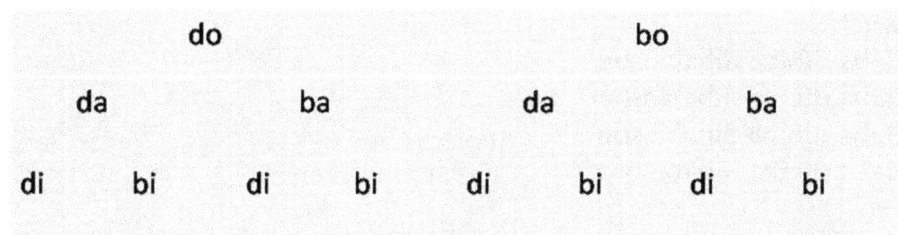

		do				bo	
da			ba	da			ba
di	bi	di	bi	di	bi	di	bi

What's an example of a dibidibi song?

Knocking on Heavens Door is an example of a dibidibi song

First Time
The dash or hyphen sign - shows notes being tied across the beat as in dibabi~ibia while the tilde sign ~ shows notes being tied across the bar line as in dibabi~osou. The | symbol indicates a barline.

Verse
so bo sadibi dadibi | dosou
so dibabi-ibia dibabi~osou
saibi dibabi-o dibabi | dusu
saibi dibabi dibiba dibabi~osou

Chorus
so daba dibiba dibabi~osou
so daba dibiba dibabi~osou
so daba dibiba dibabi~osou
so daba dibiba dibabi~uoso

Second Time
The hyphen sign - is discarded and i-i converts to a and i-o converts to io. The tilde ~ sign is discarded to create a two bar phrase.

Verse
so bo sadibi dadibi | dosou
so dibababia dibabiosou
saibi dibabio dibabi | dusu
saibi dibabi dibiba dibabiosou

Chorus
so daba dibiba dibabiosou
so daba dibiba dibabiosou
so daba dibiba dibabiosou
so daba dibiba dibabiuoso

Note: There are different ways to write dibidibi rhythmisation depending on what your phrasing priority is.

For example if you want to see or feel the bar you can rhythmise like this:

Chorus
sodabadibibadibabi~osou
sodabadibibadibabi~osou
sodabadibibadibabi~osou
sodabadibibadibabi~uoso

If you want to see or feel the half bar rhythmise like this.

Chorus
sodaba dibibadibabi~oso u
sodaba dibibadibabi~oso u
sodaba dibibadibabi~oso u
sodaba dibibadibabi~u oso

Why is this song a dibidibi song?

When there are dabadaba and dobodobo rhythms in this song why is this song considered to be a dibidibi song? The rhythmisation character of a song is determined by the lowest *rhythm resolution* within a song. In this case, since dibidibi is the smallest rhythm used, dibidibi is the rhythm resolution for this song.

Other times the rhythm resolution of a song may be determined by occurrence, this is, by whatever the most occurring melodic rhythm is: dobodobo, dabadaba or dibidibi.

The rhythm resolution may or may not be the same as the main rhythm, secondary rhythm or the tertiary rhythm. Learn more about these terms in the Rhythmisation Glossary.

Rhythmisation Glossary

Term	Definition
1e+a	The name of a rhythm counting system.
Attack	Where the duration of a rhythm starts. In rhythmisation an attack is indicated by a consonant.
Attacks	The number of sounded consonants in a rhythm word.
Attack Profile	A synonym for rhythm profile
Call and Response	A rhythm phrase where one rhythm calls and another rhythm answers in response. The phrase could be of any length, usually, four bars or less.
Click	A metronome click.
Calling Rhythm	The first rhythm in a call and response rhythm phrase. The calling rhythm occurs on the strong part of the phrase.
Counting Rhythm	A system for identifying rhythm attack patterns but not durations.
Dababa Dababa	The name of the triple eighth note rhythmisation vocabulary in 6/8.
Dabadaba	The name of the eighth note rhythmisation vocabulary in 2/4.
Dabadaba	The eighth note rhythm level.
Dabadaba Dabadaba	The name of the eighth note rhythmisation vocabulary in 4/4.
Dabadabadaba	The name of the eighth note rhythmisation vocabulary in 3/4.
Debedebe	The name of the whole note rhythmisation vocabulary in 4/4.
Debedebe	The whole note rhythm level.

Derived Rhythm	Any rhythm that belongs to a vocabulary and derives from the same seed or parent rhythm as other rhythms in the same vocabulary.
DibibiDibibi	The name of the triple sixteenth note rhythmisation vocabulary in 1/4.
Dibidibi	The name of the sixteenth note rhythmisation vocabulary in 1/4.
Dibidibi	The sixteenth note rhythm level.
Dibidibi Dibidibi	The name of the sixteenth note rhythmisation vocabulary in 2/4.
Diphthong	A co-occurrence of two or more vowels.
Diphthong Rhythm	A rhythm that contains two vowels or more. A diphthong rhythm is the equivalent to dotted, tied or syncopated notes.
Dobobo	The name of the triplet quarter note rhythmisation vocabulary in 3/4.
Dobodobo	The name of the quarter note rhythmisation vocabulary in 4/4.
Dobodobo	The quarter note rhythm level.
Dububu	The name of the triplet half note rhythmisation vocabulary in 3/2.
Dubudubu	The name of the half note rhythmisation vocabulary in 4/4.
Dubudubu	The half note rhythm level.
Dynamic Rhythm	Rhythm in tempo.
Harmonic Rhythm	The rhythm level or vocabulary used by the harmony or chord changes in a song. Debe, dubu and duobo are the most common harmonic rhythms.
Main rhythm	Refers to the most frequent rhythm vocabulary used in a piece of music.

Melodic Rhythm	The rhythm (level or vocabulary) used by the melody.
Parent rhythm	A synonym for seed rhythm.
Pataka	The triplet eighth note rhythm level.
Pataka Pataka	The name of the triplet eighth note rhythmisation vocabulary in 2/4.
Pataka Pataka Pataka Pataka	The name of the triplet eighth note rhythmisation vocabulary in 4/4.
Pitiki	The triplet sixteenth note rhythm level.
Pitiki Pitiki	The name of the triplet sixteenth note rhythmisation vocabulary in 1/4
Pitiki Pitiki Pitiki Pitiki	The name of the triplet sixteenth note rhythmisation vocabulary in 2/4.
Potoko	The triplet quarter note rhythm level.
Potoko Potoko	The triplet quarter note rhythm vocabulary.
Putuku	The triplet half note rhythm level.
Putuku Putuku	The triplet half note rhythm vocabulary.
Response Rhythm	The rhythm that answers a calling rhythm in a call and response phrase.
Rhythm Balance	Refers to the balance between phrases within a rhythm profile. For example which balance do you want for a 7A, 2 bar rhythm phrase? 7+0, 6+1, 5+2, 4+3, 3+4, 2+5, 1+6 or 0+7? Which bar do you want to have the most rhythm attacks in? The strong or weak bar?
Rhythm Density	Refers to the number of attacks — sounded consonants — in a rhythm or rhythm phrase. A 7A attack rhythm means there are 7 attacks — sounded consonants — in the phrase. Rhythm Density gives you an idea of how

active a given rhythm phrase is.

Rhythm Profile

A more detailed description of rhythm density. For example, 2 bar 7 attack rhythms can be broken into the following rhythm profiles: 7+0, 6+1, 5+2, 4+3, 3+4, 2+5, 1+6, 0+7.

Rhythm Level

Refers to the level of the whole note, half note, quarter note, eighth note or sixteenth note or triplet whole note, triplet half note, triplet quarter note, triplet eighth note or triplet sixteenth note. Any one of these values is a rhythm level.

Rhythm Phrase

A sequence of rhythm words.

Rhythm Position

The position of any rhythm event in the bar or phrase. Rhythm counting counts four quarter notes as 1 2 3 4. Each numeral denotes the ordinal position of each quarter note. Dobodobo describes the same rhythm. The consonants d and b, respectively, denote the strong and weak position of each quarter note in the phrase. You can use both approaches interchangeably.

Rhythm Resolution

A smallest rhythm level used in a composition. For example, a song may be mostly dobodobo but there are say three bars with dibidibi notes included. The rhythm resolution for this song is dibidibi.

Rhythm Substitution

Any act of substituting one rhythm for another. You may substitute any rhythm with a rhythm from the same or different profile in the same or different rhythm density, according to the degree of similarity or difference you are after.

XXX

Rhythm Variation	Similar to rhythm substitution.
Rhythm Vocabulary	Rhythm vocabulary refers to any group of rhythms that are derived from a seed rhythm or a parent rhythm. Any rhythm can be both a seed rhythm for one vocabulary and a member of more than one other rhythm vocabulary.
Rhythm Weighting	Synonym for rhythm balance.
Rhythm Word	A sequence of rhythmisation syllables.
Rhythmic Alternation	The underlying rhythm alternation between strong and weak events on any rhythm level.
Rhythmisation	Rhythmisation is the term coined by Taura Eruera to denote a system for verbalising rhythm with syllables and writing rhythm in simple English text, rather than music notation.
Rhythmisation Consonant b	The b consonant precedes any sounded vowel or diphthong that occurs on a weak duple rhythm position, division or subdivision.
Rhythmisation Consonant d	The d consonant precedes any sounded vowel or diphthong that occurs on a strong duple rhythm position, division or subdivision.
Rhythmisation Consonant k	The k consonant precedes any sounded vowel or diphthong that occurs on the third triplet rhythm position, division or subdivision.
Rhythmisation Consonant p	The p consonant precedes any sounded vowel or diphthong that occurs on the first triplet rhythm position, division or subdivision.

Rhythmisation Consonant s	The s consonant precedes any silent or unsounded vowel or diphthong that occurs on any duple rhythm position, division or subdivision, strong or weak.
Rhythmisation Consonant t	The t consonant precedes any sounded vowel or diphthong that occurs on the second triplet rhythm position, division or subdivision.
Rhythmisation Consonant z	The z consonant precedes any silent or unsounded vowel or diphthong that occurs on any triplet position, division or subdivision, strong or weak.
Rhythmisation Consonants	The main rhythmisation consonants are d, b, s, p, t, k, z.
Rhythmisation Text	When rhythm is written out in plain English text rather than notation.
Rhythmisation Vowel a	a (as in path) to indicate eighth note duration.
Rhythmisation Vowel e	e (as in bed) to indicate whole note duration.
Rhythmisation Vowel i	i (as in beat) to indicate sixteenth note duration.
Rhythmisation Vowel o	o (as in go) to indicate quarter note duration.
Rhythmisation Vowel u	u (as in blue) to indicate half note duration.
Rhythmisation Vowels	The five main rhythmisation vowels are: a, e, i, o, u.
Rhythmisations	A sequence of rhythmisation syllables, words and phrases
Rhythmise	The process of rhythmising rhythm notation into rhythmisation

Rhythmiser	Somebody who rhythmises.
Rhythmising	The process of verbalising rhythm.
Secondary rhythm	Refers to the second most frequent rhythm vocabulary in a piece, which generally, occupies less than 20% of the piece.
Seed rhythm	Any single rhythm that a vocabulary is derived from.
Solmisation	Solmisation is the system for representing pitch with syllables rather than notation. India has used solmisation systems since 1300-1000 BC while Guido D'Arezzo is credited with creating the solmisation do-re-mi system in the 10th century.
Static Rhythm	Rhythm that is written down or analysed out of tempo.
Syncopation	Indicated in rhythmisation by a diphthong duration.
Syncopation Density	The number of consecutive syncopated events in a phrase.
Tempo Rhythm	The rhythm level that is kept in the foot and is usually twice as long as the melodic rhythm level.
Tertiary rhythm	Refers to the third most frequent rhythm vocabulary in a piece, which generally, occupies less than 5% of the piece.
Tilde	This symbol ~ occurs between two vowels in a diphthong to indicate where a bar line occurs in a duration.

About the Author

I am Taura Eruera and I live in Grey Lynn, Auckland, New Zealand. Apart from a decade off in the 90's I have taught guitar continuously since 1982. That experience included teaching harmony, rhythm and guitar at the School of Creative Musicianship for six years followed by private teaching, seminars and clinics.

Over the decades I have written many titles for guitar, melody, harmony and rhythm instruction. My titles have been self-published for in-house and private student consumption or for publication on personally owned websites. Over this time my energy has been focused more on creation than distribution. Now with platforms like Amazon Kindle available, I am formatting my catalogue of work for wider distribution.

Much of my writing has come out of my studies with Dick Grove, Howard Roberts and, more importantly, directly out of my teaching experience. I am grateful to a crazy diamond of a guitar player named Clash for being my pioneer rhythmisation dabadaba student, way back in the day. Clash reckoned that his skill in verbalising the Dabadaba's enabled him to put his strumming and picking hand on auto pilot, which made life that much easier for him at the Guitar Institute of Technology.

Guitar teaching has been a major activity for me over the years. Teaching has always alternated with gigging and other activities in my work life: old school, session work before the computer; transcription and lead sheet preparation and digital session work after computers came in. These activities extended to business consultation, business startups, founding roles in radio and health care companies, software development and search engine optimization services.

Even though I am involved in many interests, guitar teaching remains an important part of my week. Writing up those insights remains an important part of my teaching..

Join Rhythmisation Insights

Thank you for reading this book. I hope you find this book useful and thorough. Let me invite you to join the Rhythmisation Insights Group.

Simply paste this URL into your web browser -- https://tinyurl.com/dibidibivol01

You will be redirected to a page where you can enter your details in the sign up form and join the discoveries!

Expect lots of useful information that we just couldn't include in this book. Expect real life resources from real people like you sharing their experiences and insights with you. See you on the inside.

Kind regards,
Taura

www.ingramcontent.com/pod-product-compliance
Lightning Source LLC
Chambersburg PA
CBHW021506090426
42739CB00007B/490